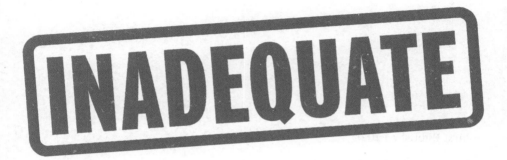

INADEQUATE

THE SYSTEM FAILING OUR TEACHERS AND YOUR CHILDREN

PRIYA LAKHANI

With a foreword by Robert Halfon MP,
Chair of the Education Select Committee

JOHN CATT

First Published 2020

by John Catt Educational Ltd,
15 Riduna Park, Station Road,
Melton, Woodbridge IP12 1QT

Tel: +44 (0) 1394 389850
Email: enquiries@johncatt.com
Website: www.johncatt.com

ISBN: 978 1 912906 22 2

Set and designed by John Catt Educational Limited

For...
My teachers, Mrs Searle (Chemistry) and Miss Delves (Physics) – thank you
My parents – my guiding stars
My children – who prefer books about Lego

Acknowledgments

Writing a book is harder than I thought, yet incredibly rewarding. For over a decade I have immersed myself in education: from teaching to working with and advising further education colleges to building technology for teachers and students at CENTURY Tech. I have learned a lot, particularly the challenges faced by teachers and children in schools and colleges. Writing this book has been rewarding, but it has also been a cathartic experience. I am really grateful to everyone at John Catt, in particular Alex Sharratt, for asking me to write what I have learned. I also want to thank Alex for his everlasting patience and optimism that he would receive a final draft despite constant evidence to the contrary.

I am immensely grateful to the extraordinary Alex Blackburn, CENTURY's Head of Communications. I love working with Alex. I am grateful for his meticulous research and for listening to my endless rambling and turning it into coherent prose. This was an extraordinary feat and I shall be forever grateful to Alex for his patience and commitment to this project.

My editorial thanks goes to Mark Steed, Principal and CEO of Kellett School, The British International School in Hong Kong, and to Harriet Power, for their invaluable advice and supreme attention to detail. I was lucky to benefit from their keen eyes and insights.

To everyone at CENTURY – the team, our Chairman, investors and our supporters – a heartfelt thank you. In the company's early days we hung a picture on the wall which perfectly described what we were about to embark upon. It said 'Let the adventure begin'. We knew that it was going to be a tremendous challenge but every step would be worth it – to personalise education for every student, empower teachers and increase social mobility. The team shows up every day, is committed to the teachers and students we serve and won't accept anything but the gold standard. I am ever so proud and grateful to the CENTURY family. It certainly has been an adventure and long may it continue.

I would also like to thank the very many people in the world of education who were kind enough to give me their time and share their experiences, challenges and successes and answer endless questions. I owe many insights in this book to you.

Finally, I'd like to thank my family: my parents, who fought for my education, showed me that perseverance and resilience matters and taught me to be fearless; my brother, I will always fondly remember being the Rodney to your Del Boy when we were kids; my husband, for his patience and encouraging me despite the many headaches I am sure I have caused him; and my children, who make every day a joy.

Contents

Foreword

Robert Halfon, Chair of the Education Select Committee, MP for Harlow and Former Minister for Apprenticeships and Skills

The coronavirus pandemic has had a chilling effect on the education of our children, especially those who start life a few rungs lower on the ladder of opportunity. When schools closed, our most disadvantaged pupils were hit the hardest. Three quarters of a million students spent lockdown learning nothing at home, especially those without proper access to technology.[1] It took just a few months to wipe out a decade of progress in narrowing the gap between disadvantaged pupils and their peers.[2] It is also estimated that the loss of school time will also result in an economic hit that will take 65 years to recover.[3] We are sleepwalking into an educational pandemic that won't be cured for generations, something that should alarm all of us – whether parent, teacher, policymaker, colleague or friend – and stir us into action. This book is a timely rallying cry to build an education system that will enable our children to flourish.

This generation of children, and those to follow, will increasingly be leaving school to find job markets completely unrecognisable to those that preceded them. From healthcare to finance to entertainment, it is clear that the Fourth Industrial Revolution (4IR), characterised by the widespread use of AI and advanced automation, is now upon us. Unlike the previous industrial revolutions, which predominantly impacted manual work, this technological advance will affect almost every kind of work from house building through to hospitality. PWC has found that 30% of jobs in the UK have the potential to be automated by the mid 2030s.[4]

Despite this early onset, Britain is, unfortunately, in a poor position when it comes to preparation for the 4IR. We already have a skills deficit, with 40% of British workers lacking the correct qualifications for their jobs.[5] The National Literacy Trust has found that 7.1 million adults in England have "very poor literacy skills,"[6] and, National Numeracy stress that only 49% of Britain's working-age population has the numeracy level expected of primary school children.[7] Furthermore, the Government Skills Survey found that in 2017 there were 226,000 skills shortage vacancies across Britain's economy.[8] If our education system does not adapt and change to meet the demands of the 4IR this skills deficit will be exacerbated and the Bank of England has estimated that 15 million British workers could find their jobs replaced by robots.[9] A further study by PWC has suggested that 46% of jobs done by young men are at risk of automation.[10]

The 4IR will impact everyone, it is not just young people that are at risk. The importance of adult learning grows more and more as each day passes. The Government does not invest enough in adult education, with a 45% cut to funding since 2009-10, and businesses do not invest enough in reskilling their workforces.[11] Those with poor education and a lower skill-set will suffer. Disadvantaged pupils will also experience a disproportionate impact and the ongoing pandemic has served to further highlight the need to protect and support these vulnerable individuals. This attainment gap must be closed and equal access to the ladder of opportunity must be provided.

Given the scale of what is happening and the fact that the vast majority of current pupils and students will enter an entirely unrecognisable economy, you would expect our education system to be adapting and developing to meet the changes and challenges that the 4IR will bring. You would also expect the Government to be preparing a significant inquiry into the effects of AI on our economy, education and society as a whole. If the system does not change, we will not be prepared for the economic upheaval that 4IR will bring. The question everyone needs to ask is 'what will be done to upskill and ready our population?'

The advance of the 4IR and the impact that it will have upon Britain explains why Inadequate is so important. Priya Lakhani has completed a forensic examination of where our education system has gone wrong. This book is an essential guide for those looking at the inadequacies of our system. From the curriculum in schools to colleges the author turns existing assumptions on their head and requires everyone to think again about just how our education system in Britain should work.

To equip our workforce and young people for the future, traditional academic learning must evolve alongside the 4IR. We need to look at whether the existing GCSE and A level system should be replaced with a more holistic and wider baccalaureate at age 18. The introduction of a baccalaureate would help to recognise academic and technical skills alongside personal development. Every young person should be guaranteed a high quality apprenticeship from level 2 through to degree level. At least 50% of students should be completing degree level apprenticeships and there should be very few post-16 educational courses which do not include a significant element of work experience.

For adult education, learners should be given an education allowance with vouchers to be spent on upskilling and education. Businesses should also get a Skills Tax Credit as a financial incentive to reskill and retrain their workers. Data from the Social Mobility Commission shows that 49% of adults from the lowest socio-economic group receive no training after leaving school.[12] It is therefore vital that learning and education becomes a life-long process. Individuals should be able to access and climb the ladder of opportunity at any stage of their life. Now is the time to rebuild our skills and apprenticeship nation. 'Skills, skills, skills' must be our battle cry as we enter the world of the 4IR.

You may not agree with every idea presented in this book. It is not intended to be a detailed manifesto. But it serves as a forceful challenge to the existing thinking that has let children and teachers down and asks the tough questions that policy makers must consider at the dawn of the 4IR.

Introduction

Let me begin with a question. What is the most powerful and consequential word in the English language? If I were to guess, you might say 'love' or 'hate', 'friend' or 'enemy', or 'life' or 'death'. But if you work in a school, then there's a good chance that the dreaded I-word – 'inadequate' – might come to mind.

In the world of education, there are few words more significant than 'inadequate'. This word is vested with the power to end entire careers, unduly branding school leaders with the label of failure. This word can destroy teacher morale, debilitate the already difficult task of staff recruitment and send parents fleeing. As the lowest possible grading that Ofsted can give a school, 'inadequate' sends a clear message, albeit an unfair one: this school has failed.

On paper, just 4% of schools in England are 'inadequate'.[1] 86% are rated 'good' or 'outstanding', with the remaining 10% 'requiring improvement'.

But this is not a book about the small number of schools that failed to live up to the inspectors' benchmarks on the day the inspector turned up. This is a book about the failure of the system itself. And a lot more than 4% of the system is failing.

Our teachers are victims of this failure, not the cause. For too long well-intended graduates enter our schools to find their passion for teaching strangled by excessive workload, their hands tied by an overly-complex rulebook and their expectations of life in the classroom crushed by the burdens of accountability and inspection. I have spoken to countless teachers who tell me that they could do so much more for their students if it weren't for the system. And these children – your children – are the primary victims of our educational inadequacy.

But to understand where we went wrong, it is important to first take a step back. Enormous steps, if not leaps, have been made in the march towards a world in which every child receives the proper education that they deserve. In 1820, only 12% of the world could read and write. Two centuries of progress has flipped that on its head – today, only 14% of us are illiterate.[2] The literacy rate has more than doubled in the last 60 years.

The rapid spread of literacy and numeracy ranks as one of the highest human achievements in history. For the first time ever, the broad mass of humans is able to understand at least basic written and numerical concepts, resulting in a legion of benefits from greater living standards and life expectancies to a deeper understanding of the world around us.

But rather than celebrating this as the final step in our shared journey of human progress, we should instead view it as a long-overdue correction of an unjust situation. Basic literacy and numeracy are just that – basic starting points from which human flourishing can begin. There are, of course, valid reasons why it has taken so long for us to reach the basics, from economic to technological. But if, for example, upwards of 80% of urban Dutch males could become literate as long ago as the eighteenth century, why do we celebrate the same achievement in other nations today, in an age of space exploration and artificial intelligence?[3] If we are to be ambitious about creating a bold future, the age of mass literacy and numeracy should be little more than basic human justice.

Despite our intellectual, technological and educational abilities reaching greater heights than at any time in our existence, our schools are still focused on achieving the very basics that we should expect of functioning humans – how to read and how to use numbers. Teachers spend most of their time imparting basic knowledge and skills that have changed little for centuries. As vital as literacy and numeracy are, it is puzzling why we still fail many children in these two basic areas, let alone why we haven't yet been able to raise our eyes to higher ambitions.

Advancements in neuroscience mean that we now have a much better understanding of how the brain learns, while artificial intelligence is enabling knowledge to be transmitted at far greater speeds than ever before. Learning science means that the process of education can be fully optimised by focusing on the teaching practices scientifically proven to have the greatest effect. Yet in many classrooms, little has changed over the last century. Most have gone from blackboards to interactive whiteboards, and that's about it.

We have entered an age in which technology, neuroscience and learning science can be combined to in effect turbocharge the process of learning. Every child can be given an education tailored to them as individuals, with teaching designed to capitalise on our new understanding of how our brains learn. The most important point is that this is not some distant, futuristic vision – it is already here and reaching more classrooms daily across the globe. Has it reached yours?

You might be a bit sceptical. As a tech entrepreneur, I am all too aware of the patchy history of technology being used to improve education. For decades, redundant technologies were foisted on teachers, often just so that leaders and policy-makers could be seen to be doing something. In some cases, technology has made the process of learning worse while making teachers' lives harder, increasing their workload and wasting taxpayers' money. And perhaps worst of all, it has reduced the likelihood of teachers being able to benefit from the transformative power of the technologies that are proven to have outstanding effects in many other sectors, with generations of students paying the price.

Scientific and technological advancements see us at the beginning of a new dawn for education; one in which teachers, students and their parents are empowered. But this is not simply a rallying cry for the use of technology in education. There are far more important factors holding our children back than the hardware or software they use. Our teachers' hands are tied, their natural passion for educating being stifled by an educational system that seeks to restrict their every move.

The coronavirus pandemic has brought home the value of our dedicated teachers to millions of families across the world. Almost overnight, parents were thrust into the roles of educators, with most struggling to keep up the pretence that just anyone could be a teacher. The pandemic has sent teacher appreciation soaring – one poll found that four in five parents say they now respect teachers more, while three quarters think teachers deserve a pay rise. Half of parents said they will now take a greater interest in education, even after school closures end.[4]

But this education system is, to borrow a word from Ofsted, inadequate. It is letting down the hardworking teachers who give their all for their students, and it is letting down the students whose entire lives depend on it.

We face a choice: once life returns to normal, do we continue to fail our teachers and children, or do we embark on a radical, evangelical mission to transform education, rebuilding our entire approach to schooling from the ground up? My hope is that this book will ensure that as many of us as possible are standing shoulder to shoulder in the fight against failure. We must extirpate the complacency and complexity that are inhibiting our efforts to improve education. This book is about raising questions, shining a light on how we are letting our teachers and students down and suggesting a constructive path forward.

But as with every ambitious revolution, this paradigm shift risks being scuppered by a lack of will, inertia and resistance from entrenched interests. If we are to reach beyond being satisfied with the very basics and create an education system that allows all students to flourish, we must be prepared to question the very foundations that support the merchants of mediocrity. The principles and systems that are holding back our ambitious teachers and students must be questioned. But most importantly, we must set out our mission – to harness both the unrivalled passion and love of our teachers with the transformative powers of science and technology so that every student and teacher can truly excel on a scale never seen before.

Chapter 1: The new operating system

'Success today requires the agility
and drive to constantly rethink,
reinvigorate, react, and reinvent.'
Bill Gates

It's probably a bad cliché for a technology entrepreneur to start a book with a tech analogy, but I'll try my best to make this the only one.

Like me, you may remember the days of Windows XP. Rumours have it that some people still use the operating system. In fact, an alarming 1% of all Windows computers still run on XP, equating to millions of systems.[1] Last year, the NHS was still running thousands of its computers on XP[2]. I've never met any of these poor souls, but if you're reading this, please stop doing this to yourself. Help is available.

On release in 2001, Windows XP was heralded as a groundbreaking piece of technology that would unlock the 'full power' of computers.[3] Microsoft put $1 billion behind its marketing and even had Sting play at its launch. For a long time, XP lived up to its promise, underpinning the turbulent noughties with a solid, user-friendly computational grounding. It started off as beautiful, simple, and very effective. Over time, more and more code was added to the system – to prevent hacks, fix bugs, add new functionality, and so on. Eventually the fixes got so numerous that the original beautiful simplicity of the system was lost, it stopped working well, and you almost forgot what it was originally supposed to do. Customers became sick and tired of it.

XP still has its die-hard fans, but the rise of more modern and secure operating systems from Windows (apart from Windows Vista and 8, which are better left unspoken) and of course macOS have left using XP more than a little redundant, if not counterproductive to a good computing experience.

Using Windows XP today feels a lot like what many teachers face when beginning their careers in our modern education system. Like XP, our schools are based on honest fundamentals – but these have been chipped away by seemingly endless tinkering. Unlike XP, the patches to education have not always been to fix important issues or to add new features, but to cater to the whims of politicians and special-interest groups with little experience of life in the classroom or knowledge of what future employers will need. And crucially, unlike computer operating systems, the complex and bureaucratic design of our education systems make it nearly impossible to develop better alternatives.

It's time we stopped tinkering around the edges. It's time we stopped applying patch after patch to education, which just means more work and restrictions on teachers. It's time we realised that if education is to meet the rapidly changing demands of the 21st century and beyond, we're going to have to start over fresh.

Our education system has been on its knees for some time. The hard work, dedication and love of teachers have been hamstrung by a system that is simply not fit for purpose. Major disruption often leads to radical transformation – and the coronavirus pandemic has the potential to be the knockout punch for our failing educational infrastructure. Equally, it risks strengthening the government's grip on education, as policy-makers feel they have to be seen to be doing something.

Before we dive into any solutions – and believe me, I'm very aware that the answers have to come from a combination of teachers, technologists, employers and policy-makers, not just me – let's consider just how bad things have become. Take the curriculum, for example. I do not think there is anyone alive, parent or teacher, who, if asked to redesign the education system from scratch, would come up with a bloated national curriculum of roughly 80,000 words. That's about as long as Tolkien's *The Hobbit*. Across the pond, the common core standards – the closest thing America has to a national curriculum – are similarly swollen. The literacy standards alone run to 37,313 words, or Hemingway's *The Old Man and the Sea* twice over.

How did the curriculum get so large and so prescriptive? In part, because successive governments, unions, and all sorts of lobby groups have made it that way. One Secretary of State for Education might want all students to learn the quadratic formula, while another might insist everyone learns the history of Britain from Skara Brae. No malevolence was involved, and many of the individual decisions that led to this point were considered individually quite reasonable. This growth is simply a natural emergent process, common to all sorts of bureaucratic systems. You see the same sort of thing in the tax code, where everyone lobbies for all sorts of little carve-outs, many of which on the face of them sound perfectly reasonable – after all, governments charging value-added tax on necessities such as food and sanitary products seems a little harsh. Unfortunately, however, over time the carve-outs accumulate and accumulate, and before you know it the nation's bakers are hiring very expensive lawyers to take the government to court in the cause of zero-rated pasties.[4]

At the heart the problem is that curriculum design has been driven by assessment: we teach what we can examine rather than what we truly believe needs to be taught in schools. A focus on accountability and international comparisons has put high-stakes assessment at the centre of our educational system. This approach has been passed down from international bodies to national governments to schools, and influences teachers to turn away from what they would otherwise opt to do if they were given free rein to bring about the general flourishing of their students. In Britain, SATs and GCSEs are largely to blame; in the US, George W. Bush's 'No Child Left Behind' and Obama's 'Race to the Top' similarly disrupted the natural process of teaching and learning.

No one would invent a system in which the inspectorate openly admits it has problems ranking schools reliably, but yet that same inspectorate has school management everywhere cowering in fear, responsive to their every whim. High-stakes assessment, of schools and pupils alike, has become not so much the tail that wags the dog as it has become a puppet master, dictating almost every other aspect of education, from recruitment to school structures. What Ofsted is to British schools, state tests and performance-related pay linked to those tests are to their American equivalents.

A bloated and pedantic curriculum combined with high-stakes assessment narrows the well-rounded education of a child. It is challenging for the teacher to deliver this, given the limited time and resources available to them. In any project or task you have three possible variables: time, resources and deliverables. In education, time is fixed, resources are stagnant but the deliverables grow year by year. Even if a curriculum is weighted – like the English Baccalaureate, where schools are encouraged to focus on a narrow selection of subjects – teachers still do their best to teach the arts, PE and softer skills, because they joined the profession to make well-rounded, successful individuals out of their students. So, as there is limited time and they rightfully want to deliver more than just exam results, they are stretched further than humanly possible.

No one would want their child to be educated in schools where a significant proportion of teachers are burnt-out and constantly thinking of leaving the profession. No one should want teaching to be a temporary job rather than a real career; a relative internship for young men or women who will teach for a few years before ultimately leaving, to spend the rest of their lives doing something rather less frustrating. A vast literature in industrial-organisational psychology strongly links worker autonomy with job satisfaction, especially for cognitively complex jobs.[5] No one can deny that teaching is one of the most cognitively complex jobs of all, as well as being extraordinarily emotionally demanding – starkly brought home to parents through pandemic home learning. Excessive control and a set of limited metrics that strictly define a teacher's success or failure strips away teachers' freedom, and arguably lowers the ability to attract and retain the brightest and best.

Given what is expected of teachers, and how poorly they are resourced, they still manage to pull off near-miracles in the classroom. But many of these are not measured, so a success to the teacher doesn't always translate to success for a school, at least on paper – and when schools are judged on metaphorical paper, the incentives for them are once again twisted.

Most people – not just teachers – are altruistic, and many are motivated by things other than money. Teacher pay is substantially lower than what many graduates could earn in the corporate world. This is a problem in itself, yet millions of teachers sign up despite this. It is devastating that they could likely get not just more pay but also more autonomy and status working for Facebook or Freshfields. On top of this, no government bureaucrat would presume to instruct other skilled professionals as to how to carry out their craft. Even professions requiring strict regulation like nursing or policing are given less day-to-day hassle by Whitehall. It is somewhat baffling that they are so reluctant to afford teachers the same respect. Yet somehow, this is the world of education.

Our operating system has become so dysfunctional that despite 12 years of mandatory education, swathes of children emerge unable to write, do basic maths, or solve real-life problems to a level deemed satisfactory to future employers. Decades of technological change, educational reform, and vastly increased per-pupil spending on schools have left us a world in which our 55–65 year olds somehow have better literacy and numeracy than our 16–25 year olds. England is the only country where this older group outperforms the younger group in literacy tests.[6] This is despite a vast increase at primary level in the number of hours dedicated to Maths and English, because those are the subjects assessed in the SATs that pupils sit at age 11, at the end of the primary phase. Nor should we forget that literacy and numeracy have been the obsessive focus of governments for almost as long as I've been alive (do you remember 'Literacy Hour'?).

And what has all this given us? The UK's performance in the OECD's international benchmarking system, PISA, has been largely flat. Many children of today are less competent in basic academic skills than their parents and grandparents, despite the fact that from 1997 to 2016, spending per pupil rose by 114% in primary schools and 90% in secondary schools – even after accounting for inflation.[7] In what other field of endeavour would we shrug at getting zero return on a doubled investment?

Of course, at the time, no one acknowledged the return was zero. After all, GCSE performance improved rapidly over this period, as it had done since at least the late 1980s. Over that period, the percentage of children gaining five A*–C grades increased from 29% in 1988 to a truly remarkable 75% in 2010.[8] Year on year, governments applauded how much better schools were doing, and of course – by implication – were able to give themselves a hefty pat on the back in the process. Very few sought to question whether or not it was remotely plausible that in just over 20 years the nation's children had become over twice as clever, or that teachers had become over twice as effective.

The improved results, of course, were largely fictional, caused by some combination of growing expertise in teaching to the test, a more intense focus on children on the borderline of C and D grades, retakes, modular exams, and straightforwardly easier questions. In those scenarios where the perverse incentives of high-stakes accountability are absent, such as international assessments or where exactly the same test is administered to cohorts of children a few decades apart, no real growth in knowledge is found (let alone a 150% increase). One study that compared the knowledge required to pass Maths A level papers from different time periods found that achieving a grade B today is roughly the same as an E in the 1960s.[9] Alan Smithers of the University of Buckingham found that while in 1982 the A grade was awarded to only 8.9% of A level entrants, 30 years later more than a quarter of students were given As (or even the new A*s).[10] This stands in contrast to the far less politically-meddled International Baccalaureate, which has seen minimal grade inflation over decades.

A similarly inflationary picture emerges from America, where high-quality data on trends in children's learning at different ages is available thanks to the National Assessment of Educational Progress (NAEP). The NAEP data goes back to the early 1970s, and assesses proficiency in reading and mathematics at different ages: 17, 13, and 9. While present-day American 9 and 13 year olds seem to perform better than their counterparts did in the 1970s, performance at age 17 – when they may need to demonstrate their skills the most – is completely flat, despite vastly increased per-pupil spending.[11] Once again, this is not what you would guess from looking at high-school grades, where grade point averages have shown substantial inflationary effects over the last few decades.

The pernicious effects of grade inflation reach far beyond the fact that they destroy the ability of grades to serve as an honest signal of achievement to employers. The constant pressure for yearly improvements in grades puts ever-increasing pressure on teachers to deliver. The lowering of standards can certainly mean that pupils learn less than their counterparts in prior generations did. The effect is especially noticeable in languages, where texts once set for unseen translation are now studied as prepared set texts.

There are also severe risks that grade inflation impairs the ability of parents to understand their child's true level of achievement. If your kid is constantly getting Bs, with some As, why worry? One survey, published in 2018 by a parent information group, found that around 90% of US parents believe their child is performing at or above the expected level for their grade – something that is hardly statistically possible.[12] Just 8% think their child is performing below average. Naturally, if parents and children are not well-informed as to the true level of the child's achievement, neither will they have any motivation to remedy the situation, since they cannot even perceive there is a problem.

All of this – grade inflation, overworked teachers, and an overfed curriculum – are examples of what software engineers call *bloat*. These trends are the ivy that is choking the tree to death, the patches that slowed XP down to a crawl and made it crash constantly. It's quite hard to stomach that decades of so-called 'reforms' led to stagnation (at best), especially when it came with vastly increased funding for schools. In America, school funding not only increased but became far fairer and more equitable: schools serving poorer and underprivileged minorities now do receive higher funding than those serving more affluent demographics, which was not the case in decades gone by. Yet the closing of the funding gap has only been accompanied by a modest shrinking in the achievement gap, even if we read the data generously. There is no honest conclusion other than that our efforts at reforming the current system have taken us as far as they probably can, and it's time to start over.

In its own modest way, this is a book that advocates a revolution. I am under no illusion that such a revolution is imminent. I am not Thomas Paine and this is not my *Common Sense*; as commonsensical as I of course believe these points to be, I have no expectations that you, dear reader, will put down this book only to take up your pitchfork. This is a book for teachers, parents and anyone else who knows that we can and must build a better system. More specifically, however, this is a book for the teachers and parents who are the foundation on which any effort at improving education will rest. A government can have all the high-minded, scientifically worked-out policies in the world, but without buy-in from teachers, none of them will work in the real world for a minute. Without buy-in from parents, they won't work either. Schooling functions by the consent of parents. When that consent is lacking, or begrudging, not a lot of learning happens (as any teacher will tell you).

Education reform, for many decades, has always been a top-down effort. Reformers have aimed their efforts primarily at lobbying governments. Perhaps there was a time when this was appropriate in the West – and indeed it may still be a reasonable strategy in many developing nations today. Even in the UK, which currently faces a crisis of teacher recruitment and retention, it is clear that part of the solution lies simply in better funding, both for training bursaries and also for teacher salaries. But government-based efforts at reforms of curriculum and pedagogy have become exhausted and played out, leaving us with pedagogy driven by the inspectorate and exam boards, and a curriculum as complicated as the operating manual for the Space Shuttle. The fundamental problem is that government-driven reform, sadly, tends to fall afoul of Goodhart's Law: any measure that becomes a target ceases to be a good measure.

While 'we treasure what we measure', it's undoubtedly true that in education, like all sectors, targets distort. An excellent example is the phonics screening check.

For those unaware of the history, the phonics check was a test instituted by the English government in 2012. The government was concerned that pupils were not being instructed properly in phonics, a method of learning how to read and write. Policy-makers were troubled by some teachers favouring 'mixed methods' of teaching reading that blended phonics with 'look and say' whole word methods. Rightly, the government took the view that the scientific evidence strongly supported phonics as the best method of teaching reading.[13] Evidently, the Education Secretary cannot be in every room to monitor teachers, so it was decided to institute a new test of phonics ability that all pupils would take at the end of Year 1.

The phonics check was somewhat unusual in that it tested children's ability to read non-words as well as real words. So, for instance, a child might be confronted by the word 'share', but the next item might be 'zoob'. This meant it was impossible for teachers to game the test by simply teaching children a stock list of common words likely to appear on the test. Children can only pass the test if they are really able to decode, not just recognise high-frequency vocabulary. This was, initially, a little bewildering for the teachers and children alike, for whom non-words were something of a novel concept, and many anecdotal reports arose of 'clever' children struggling with the test because they would try, reasonably enough, to turn non-words into real ones.

For our purposes, however, the key issue is what happened when the test, administered by the classroom teachers themselves, was actually taken. The test had 40 items, and the government let it be known in advance that the pass mark was 32 correct answers. Below is a graph of the distribution of scores of the first 3 years of the phonics screening check.

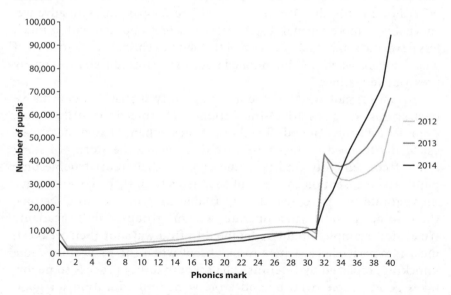

Number of pupils achieving each mark in the phonics screening check, 2012–2014 (DfE)

There is obviously a problem here. It is not reasonable to assume that the underlying distribution of ability among England's children is such that very similar numbers of children get 30 and 31 on the test, but a vastly greater number score exactly 32. One way or another, there is no plausible interpretation of this graph other than that the test was not administered correctly, and anecdotal evidence tells us it was also not introduced with enough support.

It is not always obvious exactly what answer a child is giving, especially for the non-words, and especially when the child speaks quickly and is softly spoken. It is all too easy for teachers, who are not trained in standardised test administration in the way educational psychologists are, to put the most charitable framing on a child's answer and accept it as correct, or even to quite innocently ask 'what did you say?' or 'are you sure?', thereby accidentally tipping the child off that their initial answer is probably not correct and they should try again.

Looking at the graph again, you will no doubt notice that the score distribution in 2014 looks different to those of the two prior years. This is because in 2014 the DfE did not publicise the pass mark in advance. Inevitably, a more normal distribution of scores appears, with a much less dramatic spike at 32. The saga of the phonics check is a microcosm of what happens when well-intentioned reforms are introduced in an overly prescriptive manner.

It matters not whether the accountability metric is quantitative (test scores) or qualitative (inspections). The metric is still gamed, even if well-intentioned. In those times when Ofsted has been especially focused on behaviour, we've all heard the stories of some schools conveniently finding some way for their most troublesome pupils to be absent on the days of the inspection. If the government's inspectorate wants to see glossy, trouble-free, outstanding lessons, then some schools that operate within groups (multi-academy trusts, for example) might be tempted to find ways for their weakest, most inexperienced teachers to be absent when the inspectors come knocking, replaced by veterans. The accountability process somehow takes good people, who by and large went into education for good reasons, and puts them in difficult situations where their careers rest on acting unethically.

This is simply how people respond in a world of high-stakes accountability, and you don't need to be a genius game theorist to figure this out. After all, the consequences of failure in the high-stakes accountability game can be very severe for both school leaders and individual classroom teachers. A bad Ofsted rating can end or permanently tarnish the careers of headteachers. A poor set of exam results will generally not do the same for classroom teachers, but very often can lead to an awful lot of scrutiny and pressure. The altruistic reason to try to game the metrics, especially at GCSE, is because teachers know that the difference between grades can often make a very meaningful difference to the future lives of their pupils. Yet some educationalists, such as Richard Backhouse, Principal of the Berkhamsted Schools Group, have called for grade boundaries to be abolished entirely, with students' performance being judged on percentage marks[14].

Academic opinion is not yet settled, but many scholars maintain that it was gangsta rap kingpin Ice-T who first said "don't hate the player, hate the game". Although less-frequently quoted, T went on to say in the same verse that "if you out for mega cheddar, you got to go high risk". For politicians, international rankings are as high risk as it comes, with global prestige being as mega as cheddar gets for politicians. They're effectively GCSE results for policy-makers, and instead of comparing your English grade with your mates at the school gates, you're being teased by the Finnish Education Secretary at Davos for the failure of your flagship reforms. The true problem lies in the game, not the players. We will never get satisfactory metrics of school performance unless we decouple the metrics from accountability.

The merit of international tests, such as PISA, is that they offer a snapshot of pupil performance. The tests are, however, a narrow set of metrics, success in which does not necessarily mean the country is sufficiently providing a holistic education to its students. If pupils left school successful in these measures but not in others, such as having softer skills, that country would be considered by any rational observer to have failed.

PISA tests and GCSEs are a type of *summative assessment* – assessment that is used at the end of a period of learning to sum up what a pupil has learned, often against national standards. In contrast, *formative assessment* consists of low-stakes tests – more like regular, short quizzes – that teachers give purely to understand what their pupils have learned don't suffer from the problems of exams like GCSEs. Although the idea does have considerable merit, this is not necessarily an argument for abolishing GCSEs: they do still serve a useful purpose as a standardised way for pupils to (somewhat truthfully) signal their ability to universities and/or future employers. If we are to one day scrap end-of-school exams like GCSEs and A levels, it will be because we've found a better way altogether. Later on we'll explore how new, advanced technologies combining both formative and summative assessments can meet the needs of all stakeholders.

The bigger point here, however, is that government is very often the problem as much as the solution, and when the government attempts to become the solution, it often just winds up causing more problems. It can no more effectively control schools any more than I can effectively micro-manage my employees. Good management involves trust. It also involves setting up the right incentive structure. Today, teachers are not trusted and their incentives are all wrong. It would be overly optimistic to expect the government to hand over the keys to the education system in the near future. Instead, teachers and parents must join arms with educationalists, technologists and politicians genuinely interested in long-term reform to first agree that the system has failed, to decide what it should instead be, and then set to work.

The revolution

The future is ultimately in our hands. There is no shortage of desire to change the status quo. We can see that in the sheer numbers of teachers increasingly voting with their feet and leaving the profession, with recruitment targets being missed, retention falling, and the teacher workforce getting younger and younger. Polling from Parentkind indicates that parents often feel remote and disconnected from the process of education. Only around 30% have been consulted on curriculum, behaviour management or other pertinent issues: 42% have raised no issues or offered no feedback on their child's education whatsoever in the last year.[15] Parents are not, it seems, sufficiently empowered.

The coronavirus pandemic is having a huge impact on societies across the world. It has killed hundreds of thousands and inflicted suffering, misery and grief on many millions more. Almost every one of us had our everyday lives disrupted by it and many sectors will never be the same again. Despite the perhaps historically valid view that education has lagged behind other sectors in its use of technology, some educators emerged from it as some of the most technically-savvy professionals in the world. While lawyers, journalists and even technologists have struggled to make the switch to remote, digital working, many teachers and students have taken the transition well within their strides. This not only gives me confidence that education is moving in the right direction (not because of the use of technology, necessarily, but because of its dynamism) but gives me hope that the revolution that is required is on the horizon.

Education during the pandemic is proving that teachers care deeply about the development, success and wellbeing of their students and that not even a grim virus can get in the way of inspiring and nurturing those in their care. It is also proving that something as simple and organic as Joe Wicks' brilliant daily workouts can transform our lives. This experience suggests that politicians should have perhaps long ago loosened their grip on the reins and allowed the innovation in the sector, long suppressed by targets, rules and guidelines, to flourish.

My suggestion of replacing XP with a new system should perhaps not be taken too literally. After all, when Apple or Microsoft introduce a new operating system, they are simply replacing one top-down, carefully designed product with another of the same kind. What we need is more like a wholesale shift to Linux: a set of open-source systems, built from the ground up, with anyone free to adapt and modify it as they see fit. Too many educational futurologists aim at guessing the right model for the future, and implementing that model everywhere. We must be more interested in helping to provide some tools and encouragement for parents and teachers to build their own future.

For many policy-makers this will sound rather frightening. Loss of control always is. Letting teachers and parents act freely as educational entrepreneurs in their own right will involve some failures as well as successes. Yet many of the most successful innovations in history, even if initially funded and supported by the authorities, have been the product of subject-matter experts working to meet a specific need – not the product of regulators or policy-makers. 'Necessity is the mother of invention' and, as overused as the phrase is, never has the need for a radical overhaul of education been greater. Equally, the conditions for revolution have never been more favourable. I am conscious that this might make me sound a bit like Lenin or Trotsky, but education reform has always had somewhat of a revolutionary zeal – even Michael Gove had a photo of Lenin on his office wall as Education Secretary. But far from replacing the Tsars of education with something just as authoritative and ineffective, this book seeks to empower those on the frontline to throw the barnacles off the educational boat themselves.

Futurology is a game where it is best to be very careful about playing at all, so I won't speculate overly about what education will look like towards the latter half of this century. Many of the social, economic and political trends that were beginning to shape this century have been thrown into disarray by the coronavirus pandemic. The pandemic may make loosening the established grip on education even harder, as governments across the world seek to expand their power in order to be seen to be doing everything they can to help.

I do predict, however, that the pandemic will result in people losing faith in the established ways of doing things. More than ever, we are realising that if you've done what you've always done, you'll get what you've always gotten. Sci-fi predictions of the 2020s were horribly off the mark – we were expecting flying cars, but apparently we struggle to even produce enough face masks for our doctors and nurses, let alone for the rest of us.

The ingenuity of humanity to thrive under pressure can never be understated. How this will play out is still to be seen. We could see more pressure for parent groups and educational experts to seize further control of schooling, turbocharging the British free school and American charter school movements. Or perhaps low-cost private schools, where new technologies permit lower costs, will rise in popularity. Perhaps small homeschooling cooperatives will become more prominent. Perhaps technology will dominate schools – or perhaps it will be banished entirely by technosceptics. Maybe none of these models of education will win out, and the future will look like nothing we could even imagine today. That has certainly been the case for most of history.

No matter what the new operating system looks like, it will need some basic principles to aid its construction. If you want to learn how the old system became broken, and how we should start building a new one, this book is for you.

Chapter 2: Why do we send our children to school?

'Human history becomes more and more a race between education and catastrophe.'
H. G. Wells

Education isn't fit for purpose. That, I hope, is clear. One question remains, however – what actually is the purpose of education?

It's worth exploring why we care so much about education to the point where many parents work themselves backwards from Oxbridge to figure out which nursery to send their kids to, often when they haven't even yet given birth.

At the peak of the coronavirus school closures, over one billion learners were unable to attend school; three quarters of the world's student population.[1] 177 countries closed their schools entirely, leaving just Greenland, Turkmenistan, Belarus and a handful of small island nations operating business as usual.

From home learning to homeschooling?

Before then, schools as we know them had been part of our everyday lives for centuries. But what is the place of schools in a post-coronavirus world? Will there be a rise in homeschooling? In Britain, America and many other nations, education is entirely the responsibility of the parents. Parents are perfectly free to homeschool their children, and some do. With homeschooling, it's straightforward enough to have no timetable, ignore the national curriculum, and circumvent all public examinations such as GCSEs and A levels. In the UK the law simply states that parents have to make sure their child is educated one way or another, but specifies little more.

But most parents cannot afford the time off work to homeschool, as it is now very common for the parents to be in employment, either part time or full time. The coronavirus school closures forced parents to engage with homeschooling and provided the opportunity to consider first hand the value of schooling, teachers and the benefits of schools as places where we teach our children socialisation. We have all seen the memes widely shared on social media by parents homeschooling while also attempting to work during the pandemic.

me looking at the F my kid got for the math homework i solved

Perhaps understandably, the overwhelming majority of parents send their children to a school, sometimes paying many thousands of pounds for the privilege of doing so. Independent school fees are so high that educating

your child at home – if you have time to do so – could easily save hundreds of thousands of pounds over the course of a child's educational career.

You could argue that the academic content in the school curriculum could never be satisfactorily taught at home, but this is clearly not the case. Any reasonably well-educated parent could teach the primary curriculum, and many do. Old textbooks and workbooks are cheap and quite easy to acquire, and education technology is finally living up to its promise of being able to help students to thrive.

The secondary curriculum is more of a challenge for the homeschooler, but hiring a few tutors for the child's chosen GCSE subjects can bridge the gap. If this sounds expensive, remember again that it will cost at least an order of magnitude less than the private school fees many parents do pay for. Plenty of parents with children at state schools employ tutors, supplementing their children's schooling in the shadow education market. Homeschooling also enjoys the considerable advantages of tiny class sizes, a nurturing educational environment, personalisation of the curriculum, and a flexible timetable.

So the question remains – why are schools so popular? Why do so many parents make their children attend them, even when they don't have to? What are they hoping their children will achieve at school – particularly if many feel that the education system is not fit for purpose? And with the rise in edtech, are schools and their teachers becoming redundant?

The power of good teachers

Most people hear 'educational technology' and think of children plugged into machines all day, learning in some virtual reality, with rules constructed by smart algorithms. In this dystopian vision, the humble teacher has been consigned to the dustbin of history, along with other curiosities such as the horse and cart, blancmange and the Blackberry. The edtech entrepreneur is the herald of this glorious future, who by the power of a whip-smart TED talk and venture capital money will elevate education from the Stone Age, the dreamers say.

Naturally, this is nonsense. The idea is science fiction. Even in some alternative universe where it was technologically possible, parents would vote with their feet. Socialisation plays a big role here, but I believe parents choose schools primarily because they want their children to be taught by teachers. There are few parents who cannot remember at least one great teacher from their childhood; a figure who inspired them and who dramatically shaped the course of their lives. For me, it was Miss Delves and Mrs Searle, my physics and chemistry teachers. They pulled me aside and told me that I could achieve whatever I aspired to, if I put the effort in and worked hard. Those few words influenced me greatly; Mrs Searle opening up the chemistry lab every lunchtime so that I could work on my chemistry practical allowed me to go the extra mile, knowing that I had her support.

Even parents who themselves had a fairly miserable time at school overall can often recall the teacher who helped them at their lowest point. Parents believe in teachers and the value they can bring to their children.

Indeed, in reality, parents generally find their expectations of teachers are fulfilled. Polling tends to show that parents of school-age children have higher satisfaction with teachers and schools than the general public does. The British public rates its teachers highly by European standards, agrees that they are underpaid, nearly universally views teachers as caring and empathetic, and is moderately satisfied with the education system as a whole.[2]

Polling is not the only evidence of the generally high regard in which teachers and the teaching profession are held. A quick examination of popular culture is illuminating in this regard. The bond between teacher and child lies at the heart of popular films (*Dead Poets Society*), famous plays (*The History Boys*) and the most popular fiction series of the last few decades (*Harry Potter*). Taking a broader view, we find wise mentors at the heart of great epics such as *Star Wars* (Obi-Wan Kenobi and Yoda), *Lord of the Rings* (Gandalf), and *The Matrix* (Morpheus). Some kind of teacher figure is so common in ancient mythology that 'meeting with the mentor' is regarded as one of the key stages in the structure of the 'hero's journey' narrative archetype, known as the monomyth. The word 'mentor' is taken directly from the name of a character in Homer's *Odyssey*; Mentor is an older man of years and wisdom whom Odysseus leaves to guide and guard his son, Telemachus, while Odysseus is away fighting the Trojan War.

Overall, we can fairly say that our culture loves and respects its teachers, even if this is not always mirrored in government policy. There is of course always room for improvement. Perhaps it would be better if teachers in Britain and America enjoyed the same level of respect as their Chinese counterparts do. A worrying number of parents think well of teachers but would not want their own children to become one. The status of the profession is relatively high, and teachers are trusted, but the respect accorded to other professions (such as doctors) is substantially higher. Yet overall the evidence is quite compelling that a high view of teachers, their competence and personal qualities alike, drives a good deal of the popularity of schooling.

The purpose of schooling

The teacher-child relationship is commonly understood as the arena in which the child is shaped and formed. But to what end? On this question there are a number of varying opinions. Even if we have satisfactorily answered the question of why parents opt for schools over other alternatives, we have not answered the subtly different question of what parents, and society as a whole, expect children to learn once they have passed through the school gates. The fundamental purpose of education is frequently and endlessly contested.

In modern times, one of the most popular arguments in policy-making circles is that education's purpose is to equip children for the labour market. This utilitarian way of thinking has a long history, going back to at least the nationalist reforms of the 18th and 19th centuries. In an era where schools had traditionally been heavily influenced by religion, nation-builders with imperial aspirations sought to make education far more practical. The population was to be shaped and moulded to suit the interests of the state. Education in mechanics, gunnery and engineering was to replace Latin and Greek. The 20th century saw a divergence in the purpose of education largely along class lines, with the lower classes being encouraged to take up vocational training, while the middle and upper classes were favoured for more intellectual pursuits.

Attention was increasingly being paid to what has been recently termed 'social justice' – put plainly, the belief that everyone, no matter their background, should be given the chance and means to achieve whatever they so desire. From grammar schools to the pupil premium, educational attention has been increasingly focused on raising up those at the bottom, and rightly so.

In the process, governments became increasingly interested in education, putting their financial muscle and power behind it. This in turn helped to professionalise the teaching profession. The curriculum expanded to include modern languages and the sciences. Mass literacy, in particular, was a huge boon that fuelled an enormous amount of economic growth in the years after the Industrial Revolution. The 'why' of education from the government's perspective is clear – to produce better citizens, better workers able to contribute to the economy and to respond to the electorate's democratic demands for better public services.

Nevertheless, the age of utilitarian education is clearly having a violent encounter with the law of diminishing returns. One result is the modern insistence on shoehorning ever more supposedly useful things into the curriculum. That there are only so many hours in the week is apparently irrelevant. It does not matter that everything added to the curriculum means less time for something else. The question of whether or not schools are the best place to learn about certain subjects never arises. All that matters to the promoters of utility is their own pet cause. From MPs, charities and quangos alike flows an endless stream of proposals for schools to be compelled to teach, including jazz appreciation, how to sleep, yoga, Norse mythology, how to hold a knife and fork, gambling, live-streaming and comedy.

All of these are entirely real suggestions, often from prominent figures. In 2018 alone, campaigners logged a grand total of 213 such proposals that made the national press.[3] Hundreds – probably thousands – of extra hours of teaching time would be required to cover all of them. This silliness is a fundamental indicator that we have no focus and lack a shared long-term vision for what schools are for, beyond a broad idea of using them to fix social problems we have no other idea how to solve. Teachers are in danger of becoming social workers with interactive whiteboards.

This line of thinking suggests not only that some of us no longer understand what teachers are for, but that we no longer understand education as a project undertaken by society as a whole, not just by schools. Some of the proposals have merit, especially those that seek to help children in families or communities that lack the resources or ability to tackle these issues. This includes issues surrounding mental and physical health, safeguarding, domestic abuse and careers guidance. But the avalanche of proposals has blurred the lines between personal and governmental responsibility. The self-interested calls for yoga and video gaming in schools tarnish the valid calls that would genuinely be a good use of limited school time.

One side effect of focusing on utility is that children can be left wondering why they are doing what they are doing in school. If children understand that education is primarily supposed to teach them useful things, they rapidly start to question why so much of what they are taught might not demonstrate an immediate function. They perceive that their parents generally do not use quadratic equations in real life, or write essays on Macbeth, or even speak in foreign languages, and begin to wonder why they are being taught these things. The response is often something along the lines of 'you need to pass these exams so you can get a job' – surely the most dispiriting catchphrase ever uttered in education. The beautiful art of education becomes dangerously close to slipping into a mundane chore for everyone involved. Surely we can justify education in a better way.

Politicising education

Education is not purely a utilitarian project. Teachers are not straightforward skill providers, nor substitute parents. Yet the initial question of education's purpose remains elusive and unanswered.

The philosophical answers to this question have become increasingly ideologically split, with education becoming as political and polarised as any other aspect of public life. These views, as with anything that borders on the political, can be placed on a broad left-to-right scale. (It is worth mentioning that I have found that people's educational views often have no relation to their broader political outlook – many of those in favour of 'traditional' teaching, for example, are staunch supporters of a robust welfare state and redistributive taxation.)

The educational 'left' believes broadly in the autonomy and primacy of the child. It believes that education should be child-centred, with teachers acting as facilitators for the child's own discovery, rather than a figure of authority imposing their authority and superiority. Discipline and rules are oppressive social constructs that deny the inherent goodness of the child – poor behaviour is simply the result of a lack of understanding on the adults' part. It eschews the primacy of 'knowledge', which instead serves as a transition to higher abilities such as critical thinking or teamwork. It believes that education should consider a child's socioeconomic background, with factors like poverty and class being responsible for much of a child's development.

On the other side, the 'right' believes in the supremacy of knowledge, that discipline and order are vital to educational success, and that teachers should act as leaders and figures of authority, both in terms of behaviour and wisdom. Structurally, the educational 'right' diverges between libertarians who favour school choice, school autonomy and freedom, and traditionalists who don't mind if all schools are forced to be the same, as long as they approve of the model – which usually includes some form of academic selection.

Parent readers might be surprised to learn of the fierce ideological debates raging within education. To the vast majority of the population, and most teachers, politics should stay well away from the sacred ground of the classroom. Indeed, very few educationalists, particularly teachers, fall at either end of the right–left scale. Most lie somewhere in the centre, analysing each principle on its own merits and choosing their own suite of beliefs. But if we are to answer 'why education?', we have to consider the ideological forces that have pushed education into the state it is in today. Their power cannot be understated. They are the formidable forces that left Education Secretary David Blunkett – a Labour politician – and his guide dog trapped in a room for half an hour when visiting the National Union of Teachers conference, at the pleasure of protesting militant trade unionists.[4]

As soon as you open your mouth with an idea for an educational reform, no matter how innocuous, many immediately place you in a political camp. This is a massive hurdle for anyone interested in improving education. Few readers will have read the preceding paragraphs without certain politicians, educationalists and TED talkers popping into their mind. If our answer to the purpose of education is to be relevant, it must take these schools of thought into account.

But setting out your stall in either camp is not in line with the dynamism of the modern world. Neither left or right is ready for the unprecedented social changes that loom thanks to technology and artificial intelligence. What's more, the ultimate 'customers' of schooling are children and their parents – but how many parents do you know of who, when choosing their child's schools, enquire as to how strictly Miss Smith adheres to Seymour Papert's constructionist theory of learning? This isn't to suggest that there is no place for educational philosophy. Instead, we need to decouple educational reform from ideology.

In her recent book *Slaying Goliath*, education historian and New York University professor Diane Ravitch announced the 'death' of the education reform movement. This was presented as an objective analysis of the stagnating attempts to improve education. But Diane's moderate language masked what was simply yet another attack on her ideological opponents. *The New York Times* advised that it would be wise for her to recover her former 'admirable intellectual practices':

> But even if Ravitch has often been justified in raising alarms, it's painful to see the absence of nuance she exhibits here. Those who take part in the education reform movement – a staggeringly wide range of individuals, from young people who join Teach for America to principals of innovative charter schools and officials of philanthropic foundations – are without exception malign and corrupt, while those on the other side, who have what Ravitch deems a 'genuine connection to education', are pure and selfless.[5]

This is one of many examples of how muddy the school reform waters have become and how detached they are from the view of everyday teachers and parents. This isn't confined to the 'left' – the accusation occasionally levelled by some on the 'right' that teachers and unions are solely interested in their own interests is equally unhelpful.

What do the parents think?

The educational culture warriors have entrenched the view that these divisions are set in stone and that you are either *for* or *against* them. Yet parents simply want their children to receive a good education. They want them to be able to fulfil their potential in a rapidly changing world. They just want schools to work as they should. Sadly, parents are often voiceless in these debates, let alone empowered to influence their schools.

When we ask parents how they actually feel, the results are stark. Two thirds of UK parents say that their biggest fear for their child is that they will finish school unable to find a job. Half of parents feel stressed over their child's education and a massive 80% feel the education system is inadequate for the 21st century.[6]

Parents also seem to have instincts that defy the conventional wisdom of the educational elites. One study found little connection between performance in international rankings like PISA and how good parents feel their child's education is – South Korean and Japanese parents are among the least confident in their child's learning, despite their countries excelling in the PISA rankings.[7] Perhaps Mother really does know best.

Both classroom teachers and parents – with their unique views of education as both frontline practitioners and its primary consumers – are almost entirely excluded from the 'why' of education. They are crowded out from the decision-making process by powerful politicians and well-funded interest groups. The system itself is also unintentionally designed in a way that is incapable of receiving and considering feedback and data from the frontline. This is the opposite of how any successful operation works. This is in fact one of the most common features of any failed system – think of the plethora of infamous military disasters resulting from lofty generals ignoring the experiences of their soldiers, or even of film, book or album sequels that strayed too far beyond what made their predecessors so successful. Our modern, failed education system is therefore the equivalent of *Home Alone 3*, and not because the life of a teacher is akin to being left to fend for oneself. Our policy-makers are in danger of losing sight of what parents actually want from education.

What should our focus be on?

Schools should provide children with opportunity and choice when they leave formal education. This includes a solid knowledge base, but also the skills, attitudes and characteristics that will help them succeed. They require solid citizenship skills, as well as the resilience and tools to deal with new challenges, such as mental health issues, social media, automation of jobs in certain sectors, and further unknown challenges on the horizon. Above all, kids should be safe and happy.

Schools should be a positive force in the lives of their teachers, students and parents. Children should want to go to school – not because they are placated with unproductive 'fun' activities, but because they understand the value of school and are motivated to learn. Children should love school, not fear it. In 2019, almost half of all British schoolchildren say they felt worried about returning to school after the summer holidays.[8] Even cultures with far stricter attitudes to education are suffering. In Japan, child suicides triple on the 1st of September, when schools return.[9] Japanese children are increasingly refusing to go to school out of fear, a phenomenon known as 'futoko'. As absenteeism from schools has increased, so has the demand for Japanese schools that focus on freedom and individuality.[10] Taking a bulldozer to the timetable is not a sensible approach for schools to adopt en masse. This is a multifaceted problem – school bullying and the role of parents must also be considered. But this experience highlights a wider trend of how education systems are increasingly failing to motivate our children – and how we must create new systems that are fit for purpose.

Delivering this is far more complicated than I make it out to be, and I do not claim to have all of the answers. But in the chapters that follow I will set out where we have gone wrong, and what we can do to correct this. What will become clear is that creating a system which works will involve stopping doing more things than we start doing. An analogy to this can be found in the kitchen – dishes are rarely improved by adding every herb and spice you can get your hands on; often the opposite is true. We need to pare back education, get the barnacles off the boat and let our teachers and their natural passion for teaching thrive. The narrow focus of the curriculum leaves little room for teachers to act as mentors and coaches to allow children to explore and be curious. The rigidity of mandatory targets and policies tie the hands of teachers, who, if freed, would be able to provide an educational experience far more in line with what parents want and children need. The seemingly endless piecemeal approach to education policy, in which specific issues are fixed in isolation, rather than as part of a holistic package that engenders a direction of travel and purpose in the sector, further prevents us from addressing children's needs.

In 2002, US Defense Secretary Donald Rumsfeld infamously said:

> There are known knowns. There are things we know that we know. There are known unknowns. That is to say, there are things that we now know we don't know. But there are also unknown unknowns. There are things we do not know we don't know.[11]

Behind the clunky language lies a useful way of categorising problems. So far we have looked at known knowns – obstacles to a better education system that can be identified. Yet perhaps the biggest challenges we face are known unknowns and unknown unknowns – the effects of looming radical technological revolutions on our society and economy. Let's consider some of those.

Chapter 3:
Graduating in 2030

'We must recognize that no amount of formal planning can anticipate changes such as globalization and the information revolution... Does that mean that you shouldn't plan? Not at all. You need to plan the way a fire department plans. It cannot anticipate where the next fire will be, so it has to shape an energetic and efficient team that is capable of responding to the unanticipated as well as to any ordinary event.'[1]

Andrew S. Grove

Children in primary school today will be looking for work in the 2030s. What knowledge and skills will they need in order to succeed?

History is littered with examples that demonstrate that predicting the future is a futile task. 'Heavier-than-air flying machines are impossible', said Lord Kelvin, president of the British Royal Society in 1895.[2] In

1878, the Chief Engineer of the British Post Office said that we won't need telephones because 'we have plenty of messenger boys'. Napoleon Bonaparte, one of the greatest military strategists of all time, dismissed the idea of steam-powered ships as 'nonsense'. In 1933, those who predicted the ability to source power from the splitting of atoms were described as 'talking moonshine' by Ernest Rutherford – himself the father of nuclear physics.[3] If a Nobel Laureate can't predict the future of his own field of expertise, what hope do we have?

Nevertheless, projections and statistical models can give us a broad idea of what the class of 2030 might be up against. But these predictions are numerous, and by definition, they cannot all be right. Everyone shares a desire for an education system that imparts skills fit for the 21st century – the problem is that no one can seem to decide what these skills are. Do we need to teach all our pupils Mandarin? Or how about coding? What about mathematics and engineering? All these ideas have enjoyed popularity at various times, and the coding mania got so far as to force a complete rewrite of the English computing curriculum for primary schools, forcing teachers up and down the land to learn how to program kicking a football in Scratch.

One aspect of the future that is generally agreed on, however, is that automation – using machines to do previously human-led tasks – is going to radically change the nature of employment, and thus the skills required to gain it. Consulting giant McKinsey predicts that automation will destroy up to 800 million jobs by 2030.[4] To put that in perspective, there are roughly 3.5 billion workers in the world.[5] As automation tends to be deployed industry-wide, affected workers will likely also be seeking a job in a whole new industry, which will likely demand different skills.

For a while, many privileged commentators dismissed these concerns, haughtily suggesting that displaced 50-year-old West Virginian coal miners should simply 'learn to code'. Joe Biden told a New Hampshire rally that 'anybody who can go down 3,000 feet in a mine can sure as hell learn to program'.[6] Naturally, many have not taken well to this edict. In 2019, when BuzzFeed and other media outlets laid off thousands of staff, social media users turned this refrain back onto the jobless journalists – the 'learn to code' abuse prompted Twitter to ban any accounts using the phrase, even in jest.[7] Loftiness and gall aside, programming, especially more basic coding, is itself one of the types of job most vulnerable to automation.

The good news is that automation's effect should be one of creative destruction, rather than sheer annihilation. McKinsey predicts that up to 890 million new jobs will be created by 2030, with the openings created by rising incomes, increased healthcare demands, investment in technology and energy transitions, among other causes.[8] In the nearer future, in 2018 the World Economic Forum predicted that automation may destroy 75 million jobs by 2022, but 133 million new jobs will be created as industries adapt to new roles for both machines and humans.[9]

But this is not just a numbers game. Even if automation does create more jobs than it destroys, many of these jobs will be radically different to those of today. Technology is rendering entire professions and vocations redundant. This radical change will likely be an 'incremental transformation, rather than an overnight revolution', but the final result will be the same: work will look radically different to how it does today.[10] Any job that consists of repetitively spotting patterns in data is at risk, just as clerical jobs were vastly diminished by the arrival of the personal computer. High-skilled work will be more about the provision of cognitively complex personal services and less about pattern spotting in data.

There will be fewer paralegals, and those that exist will spend their time on more cognitively complex tasks than is currently the case. Radiographers will likewise find that their work looks very different than it does today, as the processes of diagnosis and disease-course prediction become largely automated. Much work involved in office administration – such as proofreading documents – can likewise be shifted away from humans. Naturally, mechanical automation will continue alongside the AI, affecting a growing number of service industries. Food preparation and restaurant service are obvious targets, and indeed much automation has already taken place in these sectors, as you can see on any visit to McDonalds.

Importantly, however, technology expands the kinds of work humans can do. The nature of humanity is that, for better or worse, there is virtually no limit to the products humans can demand and consume. The science fiction of the 1960s did not foresee that, 60 years later, many children would aspire to be professional e-gamers or some other type of content creator, earning money through YouTube advertising revenue or Twitch subscriptions; for that matter, no one envisaged YouTube or Twitch. Even in 2005, how many thought that the celebrities of the future would be Pewdiepie and his ilk? It turns out that there are huge markets for products we never once dreamed could exist. Automation shifts human labour into radically new, service-oriented, somewhat cognitively more complex domains, but plenty of fairly low-skilled work remains and the demand for humans remains extremely high – employment in the UK was at record levels before lockdown started.[11]

Yet despite all of this change, our schools look largely the same as they did 100 years ago. We require a significant transformation in both what children do at school and how they do it. Technology can play a role in this. As we will discuss later, AI's potential is not just destructive – AI is already being used to rapidly upskill children, as well as workers, by analysing their gaps in knowledge or skills and tailoring education to them as individuals. But technology alone will not solve the problem. Our whole approach to education needs a radical overhaul if today's children are to meet the demands of tomorrow.

The knowledge vs skills debate

What skills will be required of these children? 'Skills' itself has become a loaded term. A mere mention of the word is enough for one camp of the education culture warriors outlined in the previous chapter to reach for their rifles. Their scepticism is not wholly without merit. There exist skills fanatics who eschew any need for knowledge, as 'you can just Google it'. I once even met a serious educationalist who claimed that children don't need to learn how to write, as they can just use their phones instead. Every hour spent learning knowledge is an hour that could be spent finessing the ability to use externally held information in a skilful way, they claim. In the modern world, knowledge evolves far too quickly for humans – let alone schoolchildren – to keep track, so we shouldn't waste our time trying.

Yet these arguments are rarely based on fact and often instead reflect deeper ideological beliefs, such as a figure of authority passing on knowledge being a form of social oppression. Evidence that disproves the skills fanatics' positions is mounting. As Tim Oates of Cambridge Assessment points out, the anti-knowledge camp 'fails to recognise that fundamental paradigm shifts appear very infrequently in disciplines'.[12] In geography, the last fundamental change was tectonic plate theory in the 1960s. Since then, emphases on human geography and climate issues have increased, but little else. Similarly, Oates points out that the field of genetics, despite modern clinical developments, is still rooted in Mendel's foundations of 1863.

Recent findings in neuroscience also support the importance of knowledge in education. For example, cognitive load theory posits that our working memory can only handle a limited amount of information at any one time. MIT's professor Frederick Reif states that 'the cognitive load involved in a task is the cognitive effort (or amount of information processing) required by a person to perform this task'.[13] It is quicker and more efficient to retrieve information from the long-term to the working memory than it is to constantly have to add new information to the working memory, which as we just read is limited. As knowledge is information committed to the long-term memory, a knowledge-heavy education may allow humans to perform tasks of greater complexity at greater speeds – almost the definition of proficiency.

In his excellent book on cognitive science in the classroom, psychologist Daniel T. Willingham suggests that it is a fundamental cognitive principle that 'factual knowledge precedes skill'.[14] The implication of this principle for teachers is that 'it is not possible [for students] to think well on a topic in the absence of factual knowledge on the topic'. To consider this in practice, imagine trying to fix your toilet with no plumbing expertise. I've tried – it's hard, but doable. You can figure it out eventually, with the help of YouTube and your Dad, but you are far slower than a knowledgeable plumber. What's more, with a lighter cognitive load, the plumber's mind is freed to consider more complex and creative thoughts, such as how to build a toilet that won't break in the first place, as he is not bogged down by the minutiae of cisterns, flushes and valves.

On the flipside, the knowledge camp sometimes mischaracterises the nature of the skills that the skills camp seek to promote. In a thought-provoking blog, the brilliant educationalist Daisy Christodoulou points out the linguistic manipulation at play in the knowledge vs skills debate.[15] Daisy suggests that being a 'skilled mathematician' actually means someone who has committed certain knowledge to their memory and has practised retrieving it until they can be described as displaying 'skilled performance'. While I do not disagree, this does not get to the heart of what skills are – a skill is not synonymous with proficiency, even if we do use the two terms interchangeably in common parlance.

How knowledge and skills will change

It is, of course, impossible to say exactly what knowledge and skills will be required in the future. But there will almost certainly be particular knowledge that will be of benefit to the 2030s' jobseeker. We can't predict this with accuracy, but we can and should design an education system that is nimble and agile enough to be able to react to new requirements.

What we can fairly confidently say is that future employees will still require a solid foundation of knowledge in at least maths, English and science. The study of history will still be as valuable then as it has always been throughout the ages – or potentially even more so in a world flooded with contradictory information, as the evaluation of sources is a primary skill in the historian's toolkit. Foreign languages, geography, the arts and the rest will all be just as important as they are today. While our circumstances will change, human nature will not, and these areas of interest will be as useful for humanity in 2050 AD as they were in 50 BC.

While technology can regurgitate information on demand, it is the identification of the valid information and its subsequent application that is powerful. The difference between artificial and human intelligence is our ability to understand concepts and apply them, altering their contexts, inferring additional information, and deducing motivations and emotions. While these may theoretically be possible by a machine, the demand for human, emotional intelligence will never fade.

But the unprecedented changes to the nature of employment will require new abilities that transcend knowledge or traditional skills, including the ability to adapt to unusual environments and to learn how to learn. A parliamentary report proposes an admittedly clunky update to the popular maxim on self-sufficiency, paraphrased as: 'Give a man knowledge, and you feed him for a day. Teach the man how to learn, and you feed him for a lifetime.'[16]

The goal of what I refer to as 'learning agility' is to constantly develop and grow, in terms of knowledge, skills, abilities and traits. It is to instil a belief in education that looks beyond the coming exam and towards a future in which constant change is the new norm. As the report says, the coming generations must be 'prepared for the uncertainties they will face in their futures'. The business strategist Arie de Geus said that 'the ability to learn faster than your competitors may be the only sustainable competitive advantage.'[17] If it seems cutthroat to apply such ruthless business language to the future of our children, consider how you would feel if they weren't prepared for what lies ahead of them.

Up to 14% of workers will need to change 'occupational categories' by 2030 – that's not just getting a new job, but beginning a new path entirely.[18] Even today, the notion of a 'job for life' seems as anachronistic as a cassette player in a Tesla For our children, the notion of an 'occupation for life' will likely become similarly bizarre. As the rate of societal change increases, so will the rate at which occupations become extinct. The education system must prepare young people for life in this unpredictable world. For these and other reasons, I worry deeply for the future of young people – not just for their jobs, but for their mental health, which is heavily influenced by both their material conditions and their feeling of reward and satisfaction.

We must be preparing our young people for a world in which many traditional career paths have been closed. But as Yuval Noah Harari puts it, "the crucial problem isn't creating new jobs. The crucial problem is creating new jobs that humans perform better than algorithms".[19] The in-demand roles of the future, and those most likely to escape automation, will include so-called 'hybrid jobs'. These are roles that combine multiple traditional disciplines or skill sets, such as a digital marketer who understands statistics. Business analytics firm Burning Glass Technologies found that many of the 'fastest-growing and highest-paying occupations' combine multiple skills traditionally found in isolation.[20] These combined skills often span both the technical and creative spheres – meaning the future belongs to front-end developers who also understand user experience and design. Burning Glass found that jobs with high levels of hybridisation are four times less likely to be automated than those with low levels.

We are approaching 'learn to code' territory here, however. Sending truck drivers on digital marketing courses en masse is not a sophisticated enough solution. It seems increasingly inevitable that hardship awaits millions of people, which has led to calls for a universal basic income to be guaranteed to all citizens. The economic disruption caused by the coronavirus pandemic is only making these calls louder.[21]

Aside from hard skills like programming, there are softer skills that will help the workers of tomorrow to cope. Not only will the most employable candidates be those most ready to learn new roles or adapt to new environments, but they will be those who are most ready to work in vibrant teams. McKinsey says that in addition to hard skills, 'creativity, critical thinking, and complex information processing' will be in greater demand.[22] In 2030, the amount of time that workers will spend using their social and emotional skills will have increased by almost a quarter, while the time spent on physical and manual work will fall by 14%.

Softer skills are already in greater demand. From 1980 to 2012, the proportion of US jobs that were highly dependent on social interaction – such as managers, teachers and nurses – grew by nearly 12%, while less social jobs, including many in STEM fields, fell by 3.3%.[23] This trend is only set to accelerate. The innovation charity Nesta highlights a growing need for workers skilled in 'teaching, social perceptiveness and coordination' and knowledgeable in the human-centric fields of psychology and anthropology.[24]

People who find themselves outmanoeuvred by machines in the workplace will need to retrain, upskill themselves, and find a new market for their talents. They will need to be autodidacts. Yet the question of whether we can effectively train people to be autodidacts barely receives any attention in current educational debates. This seems like a serious omission. Where is the research measuring the best methods of inculcating in children a certain inquisitiveness, a desire to find knowledge for themselves, and teaching them the best ways to find that knowledge? Instead, we spend too much of our time telling children that the first port of call for any autodidact – Wikipedia – isn't a useful source (something they know to be largely false). Curiosity should be nurtured, not quashed.

Naturally, in an education system obsessed with performance, where such performance must be demonstrated by evidence of teacher feedback in the child's workbook and copious observation notes during activities such as a learning walk, the idea of cutting children loose to work entirely independently is perhaps a little too frightening. Taking away structure is a sure-fire recipe for very large inequality of outcome, at least initially. Yet this may be considered a price worth paying to avoid the dreadful question that all teachers are far too used to – 'Miss, will this actually be in the exam?' – surely a sign that somewhere along the line, the pupil was not taught the value of independence and creativity of thought.

Adult education, a long-suffering victim of austerity, will also need to once again be taken seriously by the government. Current policy proposals include Individual Education Budgets, worth up to £20,000 per person, for everyone to spend after the age of 18 on any form of education as they wish, at any point over the span of their lives.[25] Expenditure beyond this sum would be funded by student loans in the normal way. It is a regretful feature of policy-making that these important proposals will only be taken seriously once the problem has become too great to ignore.

We have discussed the value of knowledge, teamwork, autodidactism and adaptability. The skills required for the 21st century, however, are fundamentally people skills, and there is no one model for teaching or instilling these. The most basic of these is simply the gift for getting along with people. Schools already do a huge amount of fantastic pastoral work in order to ensure that children come out the other end as well-adjusted, pro-social people. Yet little serious thinking is taking place to ascertain just how teachers (and indeed families) should be interacting with children to prepare them for a world of confusion and uncertainty.

What can schools do to help? There are some straightforward changes that schools and teachers can make to help prepare students for a rapidly changing world. Laura Tsabet is an English teacher and senior school leader who has argued for soft skills to be embedded in the curriculum. 'We must have an integration of soft skills and academic learning, which prepares students for both their exams and their uncertain futures', she says.

'Schools should look at their current schemes of work and see where soft skills (for example evaluation, reasoning, public speaking and communication) can fit into these units.' She is certain that most subjects could incorporate these skills seamlessly 'with some careful thought'.

This is already happening in many subjects – most notably in English at secondary school level, during which students 'read a range of texts, debate their opinions with others, provide reasons, evaluate successes and failures, solve problems and communicate effectively with others', Laura says.

Far from treating skills as an isolated silo, this integrated approach sees skills delivered hand-in-hand with knowledge. Laura points out that 'the academic rigour and challenge of the GCSE means that English teachers are constantly reinforcing the importance of other soft skills, like self-motivation, responsibility and time management, and providing strategies to help students develop these skills without them ever really realising it.'

The skills that our young people need for an uncertain future, therefore, can be encouraged alongside the teaching of equally vital knowledge. Far from being mutually exclusive, knowledge and skills are symbiotic, enhancing each other in a feedback loop.

With everything in education, we should strive to follow what the evidence tells us. The Learning Skills curriculum is a programme designed by the teachers James Mannion and Kate McAllister. It intends to introduce the concept of learning to learn at a school-wide level. It is based on the premise that piecemeal efforts to teach skills won't work – it has to take the form of a 'complex, whole-school intervention', an approach more traditionally seen in medical fields and social work. Through Learning Skills, pupils across year groups learn metacognition, self-regulation and oracy through a combination of taught lessons, project-based learning, reflection and discussion.

The results of this on pupils' outcomes at one secondary school in England were assessed compared to a control group over eight years – and the results were stark. The Learning Skills cohort's GCSE results were 10.9 percentage points higher than the control cohort.[26] Strikingly, the results for disadvantaged students were 23.3 percentage points higher than the control group, suggesting that poorer pupils may benefit the most from this approach. The gap between disadvantaged pupils and their peers at GCSE level was shrunk by a massive two thirds. While the researchers urge caution about inferring causality, the high praise of the school's teachers and the lack of any other factors 'that could be expected to influence the results obtained' suggest that the improvements are likely the result of the intervention.

But Mannion is eager to stress the symbiotic nature of knowledge and skills. 'In the past, people have tried to teach skills or dispositions like resilience or grit in the absence of subject knowledge, as purely abstract, generic skills. This is mistaken. Some skills are domain-general, but they are also domain-specific to a significant degree', he says.

While research showing how one particular method worked in one (or more) schools is helpful, it is essential that we should afford schools the freedom to explore and implement what works for them, rather than mandating any one approach. Producing school graduates fit for the modern world depends on embracing the autonomy of our educators.

We should also consider the real possibility that the problems we face are exactly the same that have bedevilled mankind throughout history: how to produce young men and women that can work together and cooperate in a rapidly changing world. The only difference now is the addition of a third party – robots.

Chapter 4:
Artificial intelligence

'Progress occurs when courageous,
skilful leaders seize the opportunity
to change things for the better.'
Harry S. Truman

Today, every one of us is either living with, working with or building artificial intelligence. Because of AI's rapid development, much has been made of the grave dangers it poses. Societies will be enslaved by ultra-efficient swarms of deathbots, it is claimed, if AI development is allowed to continue unchecked.

However, the biggest victims, one could argue, are our humble journalists. Spare a thought for editors who, every time AI makes the news, have to choose from a handful of stock photos featuring a dutiful looking robot festooned with Matrix-style numbers and code, as if every development in AI is akin to the latest upgrade for C-3PO's hardware.

It's no surprise, then, that much of the public associates AI with R2D2-style robots. This not only makes the lives of technology companies harder, but contributes to the public scepticism of AI that may end up holding back civilizational and educational progress.

The British polling company YouGov runs an interesting tracker of public opinion on the subject.[1] Every so often it asks the general public a series of questions relating to their view on the potential of AI to surpass human intelligence. While nobody – certainly not me, even as the founder of CENTURY, an AI company, or even any AI academic – is sufficiently prescient to answer these questions, the results are illuminating. Despite the common refrain that we are rapidly hurtling towards an AI utopia, people seem to be becoming less optimistic about AI. In August last year, 48% of respondents believed that AI will supersede human intelligence in the future. Six months later, this dropped to 45% – a small yet significant change. The proportion of people who believe that AI will never supersede human intelligence rose similarly. A Kantar study found that only 15% of people were aware of AI affecting their life presently, falling to just 5% for those over 45.[2]

Is the public falling out of love with the AI dream? One theory is that people are becoming increasingly aware that despite technological promise, much of our everyday lives has not changed for decades. Despite the likes of the iPhone, Uber Eats and bitcoin, the rate of technological change in many everyday sectors, from public transport to engineering to housing, has stalled.

This is an argument pushed by PayPal founder and venture capitalist Peter Thiel, who said 'we wanted flying cars, instead we got 140 characters'.[3] Writing for the *Financial Times*, Thiel and chess champion Garry Kasparov argued that innovations in information technology from the 1970s to today have 'masked the relative stagnation of energy, transportation, space, materials, agriculture and medicine'.[4] They argue that despite being able to send 'cute kitten photos' to relatives on the other side of the world in an instant, fundamental basics such as disaster management have barely changed since the 1960s. That the most sophisticated solution put forward for tackling the coronavirus pandemic was to stay indoors, wear a mask (or not, depending on which so-called 'expert' you listen to) and wait for a vaccine, lends credence to this view, the heroic work of healthcare workers and the real progress in vaccine development aside.

Economics professor Tyler Cowen echoes this view, suggesting that the 'low-hanging fruit' has already been picked.[5] He suggests that many recent innovations, such as smarter financial systems, are 'private goods' with localised benefits, whereas historic innovations such as railways and penicillin tended to benefit mankind as a whole.

Many readers will recall the excitement surrounding the historic series of games of Go, the strategy board game popular in Asia, played in 2016 between the world's best human, Lee Sedol, and AlphaGo, a program developed by Google's DeepMind team. AlphaGo won the series 4–1, sparking a great deal of concern about the stunning progress of artificial intelligence. This achievement, impressive as it was, looks rather less mighty when you know that the program was trained on a dataset of Go games vastly larger than any human Go player has ever played, or could ever play. In fact, depending on how you count, the training dataset was arguably bigger than the number of games played by all the human Go players that have ever existed. In this light, the fact that Lee Sedol won a game is a testament to the extraordinary flexibility of human intelligence.

The benefits of AI

But it's far from game over for team AI. Last year, the University of Oxford's Future of Humanity Institute found that more Americans support AI development than oppose it.[6] It's easy to see why. Even the biggest sceptics would admit that our lives can be made easier, happier, more productive and more peaceful through well-designed and regulated AI technologies. Futurist Ray Kurzweil predicts that singularity – when AI enters a runaway self-improvement loop that rapidly establishes an intelligence far surpassing that of humans – will arrive by 2045.[7] This 'superintelligence' will have the ability to solve our greatest threats, from climate change to diseases, with ease, so it is claimed. Surveys of AI researchers suggest a more cautious timeline; on average, experts predict a 50% chance of us creating a 'high-level machine intelligence' by 2050, with the aforementioned superintelligence arriving within a further 30 years of this.[8]

Advanced AI promises to radically improve healthcare, with machines diagnosing and devising cures for ailments far more quickly than humans, while freeing up physicians' time to care for their patients. Transport and infrastructure will be transformed. AI will identify patterns in data and behaviour that will be used to prevent cybercrime and terrorism. Dangerous jobs like mining and firefighting will be taken care of, saving countless lives. Intelligent machines will help to care for the elderly and those in need and keep them company. If that doesn't tempt you, then how about the ability to request a personalised film featuring your favourite actors from history from the comfort of your couch? I personally cannot wait to watch *Casablanca 2.0: Reloaded* with Hugh Jackman and Margot Robbie escaping the Moroccan sands on the SpaceX rocket.

Sooner, and in more tangible terms, economists predict that AI could boost world GDP by a quarter, or \$22 trillion, by 2030 – even before AI reaches anything close to its full potential.[9] McKinsey predicts that AI's boost to economic productivity will be four times greater than that of the steam engine in the 1800s, and twice that of computers in the 2000s.[10]

AI in education

Does AI's power to enhance our lives stretch to education? Visit most classrooms today and you will rightly conclude that AI has not yet taken over our schools. Seven years ago, when I learned we were not achieving high levels of literacy and numeracy in the UK during my role advising the coalition government, I looked into the problems faced by teachers and the goals we wanted to achieve for learners across the board. I had more technology on my phone helping me to make efficient decisions on what to buy or how much to invest than teachers had in school to help them with the delivery of education. For most schools, the delivery of education has not fundamentally changed since the Industrial Revolution. We have gone from a blackboard to an interactive whiteboard and not much further. On your classroom visit you will likely find students sitting at desks that are lined up in rows (or slightly rearranged into groups of tables, I'll concede), watching an adult stand at the front of the room communicating the same information in the same format to all 30 children.

How can this be so? Education is arguably the most important sector in the world. Where is the innovation to help teachers to achieve their goals? In a system rethink, we need to embrace new tools and technologies to be able to achieve our goals effectively. We need to work smarter, not harder. And we also need to ensure we increase social mobility. Mobile technology, developments in cloud technology and optimisation for low bandwidth can help to level the playing field. We could ask for more teachers – but we are already short of 69 million teachers.[11] We have no magic wand and so we need to think outside the box.

Previous decades have seen technology play an increasing role in classrooms across the world – most notably in the learning management system (LMS) and the virtual learning environment (VLE). However, this is often where innovation goes to die. These so-called innovations largely just digitalised what already happened in the classroom. We went from literally handing homework in to clicking a submission button online. The process of browsing through one-size-fits-all textbooks simply moved online. Such technology may make savings on photocopying costs, but there is nothing truly transformative about these systems. Teachers and educators need to embrace technologies that are truly cutting-edge and test them to see what works. This isn't as simple as I make it out to be – change is difficult. But as we have seen, change is also necessary.

When it comes to AI in classrooms, we are already seeing a rise in its application. Everett Rogers' adoption curve shows the rate at which new ideas and technologies spread:

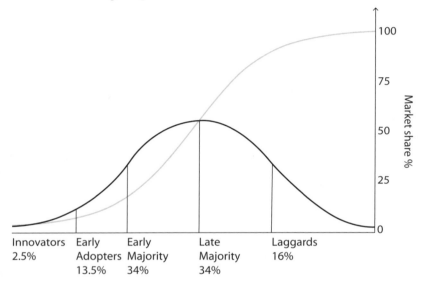

Some educators, represented by the 'innovators' category above, are beginning to harness the true power of advanced technologies. AI is starting to be used to personalise education – something for which every teacher and every parent yearns. AI is already able to provide students with an education personalised to their individual needs by learning their strengths, weaknesses and learning behaviours at a higher speed and granularity than us humans could ever do.

Each teacher often teaches hundreds of students, so learning each of their personal attributes is a difficult task, and one that is impossible to do quickly enough to maximise every precious week of the academic year. AI is now being used across the world by pioneering and innovative schools to empower teachers by giving them the data they need to provide their students with what they deserve – an excellent education tailored to them as individuals. From outstanding independent schools like Eton and Haileybury in the UK and Nord Anglia in Hong Kong, to inner-city state schools like Michaela Community School in London and the Streetly Academy and Shireland Collegiate Academy in the West Midlands, schools of all types are beginning to realise the potential of AI.

Schools can use AI to automate and improve some of the less human-dependent tasks in teaching, such as most marking and planning, often the most mundane elements of the profession. Marking in particular is an unnecessary burden on every teacher. Every week, one in five teachers spends seven hours – the equivalent of an extra work day – marking students' work.[12] Half of teachers say they would cut their marking workload by half if they were allowed to by senior managers or Ofsted.[13]

I asked Nic Ford, Deputy Headteacher at leading independent school Bolton School, about how AI is transforming marking on the ground:

> 'I would estimate that it would take a teacher an average of 30 secs to mark an average question, factoring in that they range from simple sums to longer written work. In just four months of using CENTURY [an AI-powered teaching and learning platform] at Bolton, our boys have answered 260,000 questions on the platform. That would have taken a human teacher 2166 hours, or 90 days, for the marking alone. That doesn't include the time taken to write the questions and personalise the assessment for each student, which would take even longer.'

Momentum is building – this year, the UK government's qualifications body began looking into how AI could radically transform the process of marking.[14] AI cannot yet mark every single form of work, such as long-form essays, and maybe it never adequately will. But adopting AI to mark simpler work will free up the teacher's time to focus on actually teaching and nurturing their students. That newly liberated time is essential. It is essential to be able to give children freedom to explore, and freedom for the teacher to take moments to inspire children about a particular passion in a subject, rather than feeling forced to move on quickly so that everything that might come up in the exam is covered. It is freedom for the teacher to invest in their own development as professionals, and freedom to differentiate for each student and focus on areas of concern. It could also be freedom to take a well-deserved break once in a while.

At CENTURY, we work globally and across several curricula to provide every student with a constantly adapting, personalised education. Our technology's AI learns how the student learns, adapts content to their strengths and weaknesses, and adjusts what content and tests are provided to them in order to maximise their individual performance. We also develop technology for the teacher to expand their efficacy by arming them with the data and tools needed to provide each child with an individual, personalised education. We are increasingly working at governmental level globally and are also working with our own Department for Education to introduce AI into the National Retraining Scheme. It's a happy irony that many people who may lose their jobs due to automation, as we have discussed, will in turn be upskilled with the help of AI itself.

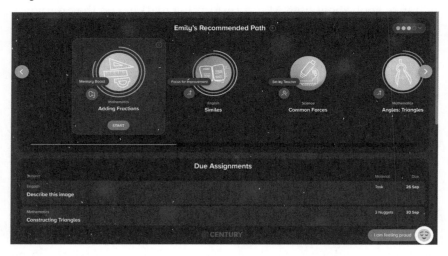

But how long can we afford to wait for Rogers' 'early adopters', 'early majority' and 'late majority'? (I leave the kickers and screamers out deliberately.) The question on many people's minds is whether the coronavirus pandemic has accelerated the spread of technology in education, just as necessity has always bred invention and innovation. Does the fact that 72% of the world's student population is unable to attend school normally, with many now using online learning, mean that even 'laggards' have embraced AI?[15]

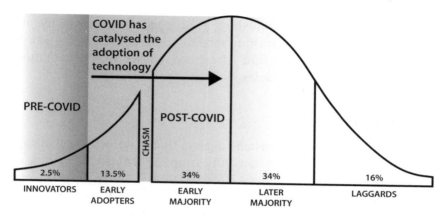

EDTECH ADOPTION LIFE CYCLE

My view is that although the adoption of smart, intelligent technology has certainly gained traction, and will grow as a result of the pandemic, many are primarily using video conferencing technology, which again simply digitises exactly how education was delivered before. When the disruption is over, these schools may largely go back to normal. The innovator-teachers and adopters of advanced technology will, however, return to a new, better normal of working smarter, not harder.

The use of advanced technology in education was dealt a blow – at least in terms of public image – with the debacle surrounding the 2020 UK exam results. In case you missed it, pupils, unable to sit exams because of the pandemic, were awarded some of their exam results by an algorithm designed to be more accurate and fair than teachers' predictions. Almost 40% of A level grades were downgraded as a result, with many students missing out on their chosen universities and becoming disillusioned[16]. The government eventually U-turned and allowed students to use their centre-assessed grades, which take into account their teachers' predictions, instead – but the damage was done. Despite the algorithm being fairly 'dumb', using statistical modelling rather than any advanced AI or machine learning, and the fact that it was not the algorithm itself which was the problem, it was the human decision-making behind its creation, this high-profile episode could hamper efforts to use future algorithm-based technologies in education. Or – on a positive note – it could simply put them under an ethical magnifying glass, with only technologies passing strict ethical criteria making the cut. This is something I have called for alongside my fellow co-founders of the Institute for Ethical Artificial Intelligence in Education. Not all algorithms or AI are bad, but we must ensure those we use adhere to strict principles.

The dangers of AI

Leading AI expert Stuart Russell suggests that if we get the challenge of AI right, it could release humanity from 'millennia of servitude as agricultural, industrial, and clerical robots', allowing us to 'make the best of life's potential'.[17] Though, as Russell would admit, it is not all sunshine and roses for artificial intelligence. The aforementioned survey of AI experts suggests that our best minds believe there is a one in three chance of superintelligence being '"bad" or "extremely bad" for humanity.'[18]

While we can currently control our AI creations, we will eventually reach a point where they literally take on minds of their own. If a superintelligent machine decides that its objective is to avoid any threat to its survival, then it won't let anything get in its way – least of all us humans. Russell points out that in this situation, we can't simply 'switch it off', as 'a superintelligent entity will already have thought of that possibility and taken steps to prevent it'.[19] Ring-fencing it in some sort of firewall is unlikely to work either, as a superintelligent machine's understanding of both physics and human motivation will be far greater than ours.

Danger doesn't just loom with superintelligence – less advanced software designed to perform simple tasks could prove disastrous. Even non-intelligent machines have been causing disruption for as long as they have existed. In 2012, trading firm Knight Capital lost $440 million in 45 minutes thanks to one rogue line of code in software that wasn't even considered artificially intelligent.[20] But incidents like this are small scratches compared to the deep wounds AI may cause. Dan Weld, a University of Washington engineering professor, foresees more danger with humans using narrow AI – AI designed to perform limited tasks – for harm. He seriously doubts that AI will decide by itself to harm humanity, but the chance that a 'terrorist will try to direct an AI system' to do so is near 100%.[21]

The ethical implications and grave risks of AI are real. But the consequences of ethical actors withdrawing from its development, leaving only those either disregarding ethics or actively pursuing its unethical use, will cause far greater harm. We must proceed with developing AI in an ethical way, with innovators and researchers bound by strict regulatory frameworks. Without sounding too much like we're in a dystopian sci-fi film, a powerful ethical AI might be our only hope against a powerful unethical AI.

We don't have to look to the future to see the dilemmas inherent in the development of advanced technologies. Huawei has emerged as the preeminent supplier of 5G infrastructure – the next generation of wireless technology that promises to revolutionise our lives. Citing security concerns, the US, UK, Australia, New Zealand, Japan and Taiwan have banned its technology from their infrastructure, with more countries likely to follow suit as the US increases pressure on its allies.[22] Some commentators suggest that Huawei is being used as 'a pawn in a continuing trade war' between the US and China, but whatever its root causes, this saga highlights the increasingly-complex technological challenges we will soon face.[23]

For all its bellicosity and bluster, the fight over 5G is a preliminary skirmish ahead of the real battles to come. Wireless technology is one thing – advanced artificial intelligence is a completely different ball game, with potentially far worse consequences. Thankfully, we are in a much better position with the development of AI. Time is running out, though – Duke University professor Indermit Gill suggests that the fate of the rest of this century will be decided by whoever is at the front of the AI pack in 2030.[24]

Britain is arguably the birthplace of AI. It is where Turing first laid the groundwork for modern computing and AI. We have slipped slightly down the pecking order since, but we have the potential to regain lost ground and surge back to pole position. It is of vital importance that British policy-makers, industry and academia do all they can to take the steering wheel and veer AI towards the technological utopia that so many of us believe we can achieve.

To put our current dilemma in perspective, it's worth taking a step back. The history of technology is the history of communication, simply meaning the transmission of information. For thousands of years, humanity's ability to communicate was constrained by strict geographical limits – the range at which the first man could communicate was, by definition, within shouting distance, or a few scribbled symbols if he was particularly smart. As technology developed, the distance and speed at which information could be transmitted increased steadily. From the written word to the telegram to the letter to the email, the speed and extent to which we can communicate has enjoyed a steady upwards trajectory.

At the same time, this increased ability to communicate has radically increased the level of interaction between humans. While the word 'interaction' suggests positive connotations, interaction can just as easily take the form of a sword as a pen. The ability to communicate and interact at a global level, thanks to technological progress, led to the growth of trade, scientific progress and intellectual discovery – but also the global domination of empires like ours, and also destruction on an unprecedented scale. The invention of nuclear weaponry meant entire civilizations could be wiped out in one stroke.

Today, technological advancements have solidified the position of the world's superpowers. Even when faced with economic and social decline, superpowers are now able to use technology as a handbrake on their fall in status. From the techno-military dominance of the USA to the oppressive internal surveillance of China, technological advancement has tightened the grip of the strongest players at the table, erecting impenetrable barriers to political entry that would not have existed just decades ago in front of their opponents.

How will this change with the dawn of AI and even superintelligence? Many argue that while transport, communications and weaponry will continue to advance technologically, the power structures that operate them will likely centralise even further into just a few hands. It is very straightforward to imagine a future in which global totalitarian rulers use technology to establish an impenetrable surveillance state that crushes opposition instantly – like Whack-A-Mole on a global scale.

Equally, others argue that technological progress, including AI, is synonymous with greater individual freedom. Artificial general intelligence (AGI) – an intelligent machine that can understand and learn any task that a human being can – could empower every one of us to own whatever we want and pursue whatever we like, as all employment will be automated, while goods and services will be provided for free.

But securing this positive future requires acting now to ensure that the development of AGI is confined by regulations so tight that they make a straight-jacket look like a flowing dress. If we let AGI develop laissez-faire, we will ultimately need to use the power of a totalitarian – there's that word again – supranational force to crush the development of a malign AGI.

MIT physicist Professor Max Tegmark posits a world in which a 'gatekeeper' superintelligence surveils and interferes in humanity for the sole purpose of preventing the creation of another, unconstrained superintelligence.[25] Unlike nuclear (and even most chemical) weapons, an advanced, humanity-threatening AI could in theory be developed in secret in a bedroom or basement, far from the prying eyes of regulators. The only way to prevent this could be to first develop an AI that is able to monitor all computer programming taking place across the world and step in to block anything that encroaches on a number of predefined boundaries. It's 1984 – but only to prevent Year Zero.

Many other scenarios are being discussed, but the point is that researchers are beginning to take the problem of AI regulation seriously. Tegmark's Future of Life Institute, backed by Elon Musk, is outlining how humanity can survive the dawn of superintelligence. Sundar Pichai of Google says there is 'no question' in his mind that AI 'needs to be regulated. It is too important not to'.[26] His only question is how. Well, quite. If Sundar had the answers to how to regulate AI, his quarter of a billion annual pay package would become mere pocket change. What AI do we regulate? Do we regulate AI itself, or just its applications? If so, which ones? And who does that – with what force? Who is punished for misconduct – the machine, its creator or its user?

When Britain's authorities can only prosecute 1 in every 100 cybercrimes, just how would we be able to protect ourselves from crimes involving sophisticated machines that are as smart as we are, or potentially far smarter?[27] For what it's worth, Elon Musk wants national and international oversight – 'just to make sure that we don't do something foolish'.[28] When that 'something foolish' includes the technological enslavement of humanity forever, perhaps we should indeed start to pick up the phone to our local MPs. Maybe we can even do a few bake sales to raise a few pounds for our local AI regulatory office. The risk of becoming a plaything to our evil robot overlords is just about the motivation I need to log on to Change.org and sign a petition.

But there are signs that governments are taking AI seriously – just not ours. Last year I asked Prime Minister Boris Johnson to follow the lead of the United Arab Emirates and appoint a Minister for AI.[29] I am privileged to sit on the UK's AI Council – and while we're doing important work, every day without a dedicated AI expert sitting at the top tables of government is a day wasted. Our national AI strategy is focused on how industrial sectors can benefit from AI, but falls short of pitching the UK as the global leader in AI development and AI regulation.

Despite Brits effectively inventing AI, Britain seems content to let others both reap the rewards and mitigate its dangers. We're the equivalent of Prometheus stealing fire from the heavens and gifting it to humanity, except we've decided to chain *ourselves* to the rock by not capitalising on AI's true potential. Keeping things mythical, the opening of Pandora's Box, put on Earth by Zeus in order to punish humans for accepting Prometheus' gift of fire, unleashed hardships and curses ranging from sickness to famine on the world. The only blessing that Pandora managed to close the lid on was 'hope'. It may seem slightly melodramatic, but unless we get serious, the creation of AI could be described as slightly Pandoran. Like her opening of the box, our pursuit of AI is based on curiosity, not malice, but we have a responsibility to ensure that we can extract as much of the 'hope' as possible and keep the hardships to a minimum.

For my part, in 2018 I co-founded the Institute for Ethical AI in Education alongside Sir Anthony Seldon and Professor Rose Luckin. The IEAIE provides a framework upon which we can reap the many benefits of AI in education, while ensuring threats to privacy and security are addressed. But our ambitions, not just as governments but as civilizations, can and should be far higher.

As I think I have made clear, I'm not an AI utopian who is blind to the many, real risks that AI poses to not just a meaningful existence, but to existence itself. But a well-designed, well-regulated AI could bring massive benefits to every aspect of our lives, not least of all the world of education.

With all the talk of harnessing the power of technology in the classroom, we must not lose sight of what truly lies at the heart of education's power to change lives – the human teacher.

Chapter 5: Our teachers

'Teachers are expected to reach unattainable goals with inadequate tools. The miracle is that at times they accomplish this impossible task.'[1]
Haim Ginott

The child is the most important person in the classroom, but the teacher is the most powerful. In theory, at any rate. But if teachers are so crucial, why do we waste so much of their time?

If you're a parent of school-aged children, you may have noticed that your kids' teachers seem rather busier than your own teachers appeared to be when you were at school. They seem permanently hassled, lost in a frenetic whirl of meetings and marking. This seems rather odd. Surely teaching is the sort of job that's famous for its compatibility with family life?

If you've noticed this, you're not suffering from unwarranted nostalgia. Teaching really has become a lot more intense. The British government has, over the last few years, conducted and released some very interesting research on the matter, both quantitative and qualitative. In the latter type of research, teachers from all sorts of different schools spoke forthrightly and in their own words. The results are so revealing that I thought it best to simply put some of the money quotes here.[2]

'It is the expectation that books are marked and the marking policy is followed... It is not just ticks. Every member of staff annotates work with specific actions that students need to do following written assessment... If we find books are not marked for three weeks we are expected as leaders to challenge that member of staff. There is quite a large demand on staff... [they] typically work until 9pm.' (Assistant Principal of a secondary school)

'We had an assessment policy [where we had to give] three feedback comments – it's useful feedback, but it's time consuming to write the three comments for 30 students after you've marked the test. It takes hours.' (Secondary school Science teacher)

'Parents now email staff directly and we are expected to reply within 24 hours. Students email and we have to reply to them individually outside of school hours, for example forwarding homework tasks or answering queries about homework. I am expected to answer emails from SLT (the senior leadership team in schools) [during] lessons I am teaching. If I don't I am questioned as to why I've not responded. I can have hundreds in a day, the turnaround expectations are high.' (Secondary school Maths teacher)

Sadly, the thoughts of the teachers staying until 9pm in the school where the Assistant Principal works are not recorded. It would be even more illuminating to talk to the families of those teachers, if anyone at home still recognised them by now.

The quantitative data on teacher workload largely concurs with the more impressionistic picture that emerges from focus groups. Full-time teachers work about 50 hours a week on average, with a quarter of teachers working over 60 hours a week.[3] The hours in term-time approach those of investment banking or corporate law, while the pay does not. While teacher workload across the entire year is roughly comparable to most other graduate professions – since teachers' greater 'holiday' time (ignoring the fact that many teachers spend part of this so-called free time planning the next academic year!) averages it out – teaching is a unique job in the cognitive and emotional demands it places on those practising it. Having to manage the demands of thirty-or-so children for around seven hours a day for five days a week is shattering. If you thought your coronavirus homeschooling was tough, imagine doing this for all of your friends' children at the same time. Teaching is in many ways comparable to professional acting. The teacher has to get up on stage and perform in front of an audience of merciless critics who instantly punish any lapse. It is incredibly physically draining.

How can it be the case that teachers report working around 50 hours a week – or more, in many cases – and yet they only report spending slightly less than half that time actually teaching? What on earth are they doing with their time? In fact there is no mystery. A re-read of the statements excerpted above from the government's focus group will reveal the solution. Teaching time has disappeared beneath a blizzard of marking and planning. The latter is more manageable for experienced teachers who have built up a large bank of lessons from prior years, or teachers in bigger departments who can share their planning with colleagues, but it is still a huge burden for many teachers in single-form primaries or small departments. Marking is a vast burden for almost all teachers in schools with onerous marking policies.

Just about managing

Another extraordinary burden is data management, with many schools requiring regular 'data drops' of student assessment data from their teaching staff. Think about it – if you are a parent who has been homeschooling, how do you know where your child is struggling? You do this by setting a test, marking and analysing it. That takes serious time (*shameless plug alert* – unless you're using CENTURY), and that's only for one kid. A life of menial data-entry work is of course exactly what all teachers signed up for, and surely the kind of thing that gives them joy and fulfilment in their work – right?

Wrong. Where on earth did these policies come from? Parents may well be somewhat bewildered, and rightly so. After all, surely when Mr Smith scrawled 'READ THE QUESTION' all over your Maths homework in 1994 (or 'RTQ' for short, or 'RTFQ' when he got really mad), he surely couldn't have been following an actual marking and feedback policy, could he? Indeed he was not. Once upon a time marking, and planning lessons too, was the private business of teachers, not something for school management to concern themselves with – as unimaginable as that may seem to most new teachers working in 2020.

This began to change throughout the early 2000s, when schools increasingly became a playground for well-meaning politicians to show how much they care about improving public services. A booming population also meant that school policies and regulations increasingly fell under the spotlight. The dawn of international rankings saw politicians fretting about how they would stack up against their elite peers.

The increased accountability of school leaders to the government led in turn to an increase in accountability of subject leaders and teachers to school leaders. One of the effects of this was to radically increase the element of management in education. I don't simply mean staff in school; management includes Ofsted, the government and a host of other stakeholders who all suddenly began to take a bigger interest in what schools were doing. What happens then? Management itself increasingly becomes the business of the institution. Good management is of course a necessity in any well-functioning organisation, but management for the sake of it is detrimental. It can hardly be a coincidence that classroom teachers began to feel themselves much more intensively under the cosh at exactly the same time as education came under the managerial spotlight.

By the time it became apparent that this was a problem, ironically enough, a very urgent need for more in-school management arose as a result of the government's academisation programme. A great many administrative functions that would once have been performed by local authorities were transferred to schools. In theory, the idea was that administrative functions would be performed centrally by large multi-academy trusts (MATs) by full-time clerical staff, thus generating economies of scale. In practice, tightening school budgets meant that a great deal of work was transferred to teachers who were given management responsibilities. All this generated even more demand and workload for teachers, diverting their time and energy away from actually teaching. School inspectors' focus on the importance of the curriculum created even *more* work, as schools were tasked with developing and implementing new curriculum models, often without much support from local authorities or their MAT.

To an underappreciated degree, I think this change could have been driven by the fact that there is no way to promote teachers in the UK schooling system without giving them management responsibilities. Faced with this problem, schools created more managers, and managers need something to manage.

Technology and the thirst for data

Badly used technology has played a role, too, in the demeaning of our teachers. The grizzled teaching veterans of 2020, who began their careers around 1995 (remember AOL?), almost certainly did not receive any emails at the start of their careers. The modern teacher, especially one with management responsibilities, may receive a very large number of emails per day, from both parents and other managers. Many poor souls are even caught up in WhatsApp parent groups. Let us assume that the secondary Maths teacher quoted earlier in this chapter gets on average 50 emails a day and that each email needs on average 4 minutes of her time to digest and reply. This works out to 200 minutes a day (3 hours 20 minutes), or 16 hours 40 minutes a week. Even if we assume fewer emails and a quicker reply time, you can very easily see how teaching – a job in which the basic work patterns were laid out in very different times – has become perhaps more challenging in modern times.

For all its drawbacks, at least the humble pigeon hole could not follow you around the classroom, out of the school gates and onto the sofa at home, beeping and shaking at you until you opened the letters it contained – and letters are indeed a form of communication that tend to produce more thoughtful, considered interactions than its modern electronic forms.

But the story of how the first wave of information technology in schools actually added to teacher workload goes well beyond email. The creation of the various nationwide school tests like GCSEs meant there was a lot more individual pupil data kicking around for people to analyse. It was, in theory, possible to work out which teachers and which schools were adding the most value. Which schools have the best results at age 11? At age 14? At age 16? If you test kids frequently enough, the same analysis can easily be done at the level of individual classrooms and their teachers. It can also be applied to subgroups of children, such as those from disadvantaged backgrounds. An unintentional byproduct of the creation of so many national standardised tests was the 'data revolution' in educational accountability.

The theory was sound enough. High-quality data, analysed thoughtfully, really can be transformational, just as it is in every other sector. In theory it is quite possible, given sufficient high-quality test data, to work out value-added scores that tell you which teachers in your school are doing the best work. This could not only be used for performance-related pay, but identifying these teachers could also help schools to learn from replicable elements of their methods. It all sounds perfect, right? What could possibly go wrong?

The most obvious problem is that the data revolution required very large amounts of data. For that, you need at least yearly tests. But yearly tests aren't much good in practice. They are too infrequent to be useful from a data analysis perspective. High-stakes testing, as it is known, is not only detrimental to the child, but also close to useless for actually finding out how well children are learning. To produce data that actually can be analysed properly, teachers find themselves conducting many more frequent tests, marking them, and inputting the results to centralised databases. On TeacherTapp, an app that polls a fairly representative sample of UK teachers on a daily basis about their working lives, well over half reported that they were required to do these 'data drops' every half-term.[4]

More frequent, low-stakes testing (known as formative assessment) should not just happen to please school managers looking for data – it is a really powerful way for teachers to see progress and gaps without stressing out their pupils or distorting the curriculum. We will come on to this in a later chapter. But already you can see the problems for teacher workload. British teachers found themselves caught in a giant trap; servants feeding the ravenous data monster. Jerry Z. Muller, a professor of history, calls this 'the tyranny of metrics' – the growing fixation with quantification that, when poorly thought out, has a paralysing effect on institutions from schools to hospitals to the military[5].

By 2016, the English schools inspectorate incorporated a specific expectation for schools to use data-management systems to track the progress of individual pupils. Unsurprisingly, within a few years, this expectation was gone, and Ofsted is now explicitly *refusing* to look at *any* internal data that a school might produce. Instead, the inspection framework has moved away from a quantitative to a qualitative framework, in part because Ofsted came to realise the degree to which its own procedures were indirectly putting an intolerable burden on classroom teachers.

So is everything fine now? Have our teachers been released from their chains? Are they free to do what they want to do – just get on with teaching? Of course not. The managerial prison in which our teachers dwell has simply changed the wallpaper. The locks remain firmly on the doors. A new Ofsted framework simply means a new form of managerialism, new hoops to jump through and new hurdles to overcome.

The school inspectors may not look at your spreadsheets of data, but now they want to see your pupils' workbooks. And perfect these workbooks must be. Learning objectives (always written down, of course) must form a logical sequence. Teachers must never deviate from a planned progression scheme, whether or not they think their children need some revision time or a refresher class on something they learned a few months ago. Marking needs to show evidence of not just assessment but also progression: the teacher writes comments in one colour, the child responds in another, the teacher responds yet again in a third. And, because Ofsted gives very little notice of when they're coming, schools have a huge incentive to make sure pupils' books are in perfect shape all the time, just in case. Fear of the inspectorate drives so much of what happens in schools, far more than their actual presence ever could.

The shape of modern school inspections is another source of the distortion field that surrounds schools. Before 2005, inspections were lengthy affairs, with large inspection teams staying in schools for a week. As onerous as this was, it did mean that inspectors got to form their own judgements for how schools really functioned, and these judgements were generally quite reliable. Budget cuts forced Ofsted to shift to the modern format of small teams conducting short inspections, which in turn meant that inspectors became much less persons temporarily embedded within a school, and more people who showed up to review the data the headteacher presented them with (since this was all they really could do). Given this, the headteacher had an enormous incentive to have lots of positive data on hand to present to Ofsted at all times, which meant yet another incentive to collect data from staff ... you can see where this is going.

The self-sacrificial teacher

There is one more perverse incentive structure I want to talk about, and it is the general moral code that teachers operate under. You could call it the memeification of teacher morality. I don't insist on that name, but I'm sure you all know what I mean, especially if you've seen some variant of this:

"A good teacher is like a candle, it consumes itself to light the way for others."

The major problem with this meme, and the moral code it betrays, is that once you legitimise the idea of teachers as quintessentially self-sacrificing, there is surely no sacrifice you cannot expect them to make. If teachers do everything 'for the kids', then there is immense pressure on them to accept anything that might benefit the children in their care, no matter the cost to the teachers themselves, and no matter how slim the gain to the children. It's such a petty example, but I always think the best case of this is all the marking policies that make teachers mark with different coloured pens. Even 'tick and flick' marking of a Maths worksheet turns into an utterly laborious, degrading chore if you have to constantly swap pens every time a pupil gets an answer wrong, and then it gets even worse when you realise you've used the purple pen to mark a correct answer and now you have to get the green pen again and carefully colour over your incorrect usage of purple, and by now it's 7.30pm and you are exhausted and just about ready to throw the blasted homework into the rubbish bin and use the pens to plot the cold-blooded murder of whoever devised the flipping marking policy.

No one makes memes like this for engineers or lawyers! It really does just seem to be teachers. Furthermore, teachers are not just teachers: they are very often husbands, wives, children and above all parents. Faced with the choice between altruistically caring for their family or altruistically caring for the bottom set of Year 10 Maths on a Friday afternoon, many will quite rationally choose the former, and you need not be a sociobiologist to understand why. But in practice, many don't have a choice – they can't afford to not choose the pupils, and end up exhausted. During the coronavirus lockdowns, many teachers have also struggled to look after their own kids at home while teaching their pupils online.

Autonomy

It is no surprise, then, that many teachers decide that enough is simply enough. Teachers are increasingly becoming burned out at a young age; a term that used to be reserved for high-powered lawyers and soldiers in the line of fire. It is not just the hours worked, though – it is the decreasing feeling of control, autonomy and reward that leads our teachers to pack up and leave. People can and do work stressful jobs with long hours in a sustainable fashion. The key is that they feel they have autonomy over their work, and that the work itself is meaningful. This is where teaching in 2020 falls down.

The teachers of years gone by may also have worked quite long hours, and some evidence suggests they did. Veteran teachers tend to agree, however, that the key difference between now and then is that much of the work they did in the days of yore was self-directed. There is a very big difference between putting up a beautiful display on the corridor wall outside your classroom because you thought it would inspire and celebrate your pupils, and doing so because the newly revised displays policy says you must. One is a voluntary offering done with pride, the other a laborious chore done to someone else's schedule. Marking because the marking policy tells you to is a very different thing from marking because you are eager to review your pupils' work and give them vital feedback, not least because in the former situation teachers are doing a lot more marking than they otherwise would. Polling suggests that teachers find marking and data collation the biggest factors to their workload, and that fixing them would improve their wellbeing.[6]

It is only when you drill down into the nitty-gritty of teachers' daily work routines that you realise how little freedom they truly have in so many schools, and polling suggests that the more deprived a school's intake, the more tightly controlled its teachers are.[7] Instead of rewarding teachers who go to work in more challenging areas with better pay and working conditions, we punish them by giving them the least amount of the one thing industrial-organisational psychology tells us almost all workers crave.

When someone else controls how and in what quantity you mark, how you arrange the chairs in your classroom, what goes on the walls, how and in what quantity you do formal assessments, what form your planning takes, and even in many schools numerous aspects of your pedagogy, how much room is there left for genuine teacher autonomy, anywhere? Do parents think the colour of the pens and the number of displays in a school will affect their decision about whether this is a safe and happy school for their child? Or would they instead make such a decision based on the quality and autonomy of the teachers?

My final thought on how things got this way is that school improvement is, given existing resource constraints, a very difficult problem to solve. School managers are placed in the position of being expected to improve results each and every year while at the same time being expected to narrow or even entirely close achievement gaps between various subgroups of children that they did not create and that often existed long before those pupils went to primary school.

What can you do when the government tells you that you must solve a problem, but you don't know of a workable strategy for solving it? Well, you can do one thing: you can always make the people under you work harder. This will probably drive some improvement in results, no matter how small and short-term, and it invariably looks good to outsiders. How can parents or Ofsted argue with your leadership if everyone is working very hard and – for now – sticking around? And of course, the general culture of teacher morality makes it very easy for leaders to make their staff work harder, at the cost of their long-term effectiveness as teachers, let alone their mental health.

Making things better

'A movement is on foot' with regards to improving the status of teachers. Wonderful news, of course – except this quote is from an academic paper from 1938.[8] Today's teachers are facing the same problems as their peers from a century ago. Teachers have struggled to gain trust and recognition since before their Biros were even invented. While it is vital to understand how we got into this mess, the most important thing of all is to chart our course out of it. We know from what works in other sectors that freedom and trust are essential. Once the important basics like safeguarding and wellbeing are taken care of, we must learn to trust our teachers. That is the only way we will get the best out of our creative army of millions of educators.

Consistency in the classroom is key. The well-meaning may think consistency is achieved with many policies and processes. However, controlling teachers and micro-managing them to the degree of which colour marker they use erodes trust, and trust is critical to the culture of the organisation and to the profession as a whole. Setting teachers free may not sound like the optimal way to achieve consistency. But the only consistencies produced by distrust are consistent underperformance and unhappiness. A lack of trust in any organisation leads to fear, anxiety, reduced morale and inevitably a decrease in performance. This is well known and avoided by good leaders in any other sector. Millions of pounds are spent annually in workplace transformation projects so that businesses can avoid such behaviour, as a toxic culture can lead to their demise.

Four in every five teachers have considered quitting their jobs because of workload alone.[9] Isn't this enough of a warning that something needs to change, and fast? In order to create trust and remove the destructive cycle of micromanagement in schools, leaders need to allow their teachers the time and autonomy to build their own classroom practices. We build trust when we see patterns of positive and desirable behaviour by others and when they respond well to constructive feedback.

We need to embrace the passion and drive in education and stop suffocating it out of existence. Take Andria Zafirakou, a London art teacher, who won the $1m Global Teacher Prize in 2018.[10] She beat teachers nominated from more than 170 countries to be named the best in the world. She did this despite having to adhere to every school, government and inspectorate policy. She took the prize 'by being the kind of teacher our education system actively discourages'.[11] Imagine what she – and the millions of other teachers equally passionate about improving young peoples' lives – could do if they were actually trusted to do their jobs.

Readdressing the dire work-life balance in teaching doesn't mean we have to reinvent the wheel. There are many straightforward organisational measures that schools can take to improve teacher wellbeing.

The world of work is changing, as we have discussed. The 'gig economy' – in which jobs tend to be short-term or freelance – has more than tripled in size in the last four years.[12] While no one in their right mind would want to turn education into UberSchool, the normalisation of short-term work is leading to a cultural shift in the way we see work. In education, this means that demand for more flexible working arrangements is rising. Roughly a quarter of primary school teachers and a fifth of secondary school teachers work part-time – rates that have been rising steadily since 2010.[13] Offering more flexible working patterns improves teacher retention, staff wellbeing, expertise retention and reduces total staffing costs.[14]

Yet while the situation is improving, many teachers are still not able to work flexibly. Last year, a report found that one in six teachers would reduce their hours if they could.[15] Another survey suggests that less than half of teachers would work full time if they were able to instead work part time.[16] Of those who could afford to work part time but currently don't, a third say they haven't asked because they believe their request would be dismissed, while 14% have already had their request rejected by managers.[17] Flexible teaching experts Lucy Rose and Lindsay Patience say that it is 'extremely hard' to find examples of schools in which flexible working has been formalised because headteachers tend to arrange it surreptitiously to avoid a 'flood of requests'.[18]

If so many teachers want flexible working, why don't we make it easier for headteachers to allow it? While schools are different to companies, with their more typical working conditions, it is surely not beyond the wit of humanity to come up with a solution. This is perhaps one area in which a stronger lead from the government could be helpful. Lindsay Patience suggests that while a one-size-fits-all approach would be doomed to fail, the government could give more support to school leaders to allow them to approach flexible working with greater confidence. In their defence, these school leaders might say that flexible working en masse in schools is simply too disruptive to the education of children. Some of those I have spoken to take the view that we should put the interests of children above those of teachers.

Do we just need to pay teachers a bit more? It is tempting to think so. The Organisation for Economic Co-Operation and Development (OECD) – the supposed fount of all economic and educational wisdom – suggests that 'high-performing education systems tend to pay their teachers more'.[19] Research from the US suggests that teachers earn a tenth less than other workers with comparable education and experience.[20] Teachers in England have it particularly bad, it seems – last year we learned that English teachers are paid less than anywhere else in the developed world.[21] The only teachers who have received a bigger paycut over the last few decades than English teachers are those in Greece – a country whose economy almost entirely collapsed over the same period.[22]

To tackle this absurdity, in 2020 the UK government announced a pay boost for both new and existing teachers in England, which claimed to be their 'biggest pay rise in fifteen years'.[23] This is welcome news that will help to reward our teachers and attract new talent, but more pay is not a fix-all. We cannot solve all the many problems with how we treat our teachers by simply throwing more money at them – it would be patronising to think so. Pay forms just one part of the solution; making teaching an attractive and rewarding profession requires a wholesale raising of the status of teaching, transforming teachers' career prospects and giving them more autonomy and agency. After the coronavirus pandemic plunged us all into the role of teacher, I doubt few parents would disagree that teachers deserve all the money in the world – but we need to do so much more than that.

My work as a trustee of the Teaching Awards Trust, an organisation set up to recognise and celebrate teachers, is so important to me. I joined because it incensed me that the profession is overlooked and under-celebrated. A bright and passionate Maths teacher working in a deprived area in South England once told me that he's 'just a Maths teacher' and thought this was normal. That simply isn't right. We need to raise the profile of the profession and recognise teachers' value. At CENTURY, we sponsored the Thank a Teacher campaign, which has enabled people to send nearly 40,000 messages of thanks to their current or former teachers in the last year.

We must also begin to fully trust teachers. Trusting teachers means no more display policies, no more marking policies, and especially no policies that treat teachers like 5-year-olds by mandating which colour pen they can and cannot use. How can you ever expect to attract the top graduates into a profession where they are treated this way? Staff meetings should be short and to the point. Those meetings which are not relevant to particular members of staff should not require their attendance. Get rid of any assessment system that requires teachers to make 'data drops'. There should be no standardised format for planning beyond the minimum necessary for other people to use those plans if the teacher works in a department where this is necessary.

Some working in leadership positions in schools may be reading this and thinking 'ok, but how am I supposed to evaluate my teachers if you take away my tools for doing so?' The short answer is that these tools aren't actually helping you to evaluate teachers to begin with, so you should stop using them. Evidence and anecdote suggest that school leaders are generally quite good at intuitively knowing who their best teachers are, and who needs help. The ones who need help are not going to be made into great teachers if you dictate to them how they should mark, plan and assess. They need proper professional development with coaching and training. And meanwhile by enforcing these policies on everyone you alienate the vast majority of your workforce, who are either great teachers or are well on their way to becoming great.

Letting go of control is scary. For so many, teachers and managers alike, professionalism has come to mean that everyone does the same thing in the same way. We all like to believe in the idea that there is one scientific way to teach, one scientific way to run a school. Everyone likes the idea of 'best practice'. There exists a very seductive notion that if only we pick the right practices, if only we ensure they are uniformly practised – only then we will finally 'close the gap' or achieve what other ill-specified outcome we have set ourselves. This notion is an illusion.

Teaching needs too many highly complex and personally refined skills to ever be standardised. The teacher is far more like the artisan jeweller than the worker on the automotive assembly line. Yet teaching is far more complicated even than artisanal craftwork, because the materials the teacher has to work with are themselves real human beings, each with their own unique background, talents and personality. The teacher somehow has to interact with each student simultaneously while also dealing with the overall group dynamics that emerge from the interactions between the pupils. Put this way, even someone who has never taught can easily see that teaching is an impossibly complicated high-wire act.

Learning emerges from a plethora of interactions between wildly diverse minds – something that is virtually impossible to properly model. At best, we can roughly evaluate the results, but understanding the details of the process by which learning occurs is virtually impossible. This alone should make us extremely wary of controlling our teachers too much, even if it were not very clear that doing so is making it impossible to recruit and retain the sort of teachers we want.

The crisis in teacher workload ultimately results from the delusion that someone else knows better than the man or woman on point in the classroom. The vast majority of the time, they do not. There must be no beating about the bush on this point. Let us set our teachers free.

Chapter 6: The curriculum

'Truth is ever to be found in the simplicity, and not in the multiplicity and confusion of things.'
Isaac Newton

Every year, in Britain alone, around 25,000 freshly qualified teachers begin their first day at school as educators. Let's imagine, for a moment, that you are one of them. You are about to be introduced to your first ever class. The excitement is building; you are nervous, but equally thrilled about the occasion, and can't wait to get down to finally helping your students to flourish.

About a week in, however, you notice something rather odd in your Maths lessons. Around a third of the kids seem to be a bit shaky on the basics. And not the basics in terms of column addition or other straightforward mathematical operations – they're wobbly on basic addition and subtraction of numbers below 20. Rather than $7 + 6 = 13$ being a matter of automatic recall, for some it involves some rather arduous calculations on fingers. Others are faster but still quite often make mistakes.

Naturally, you are troubled by this. You wonder, secretly, if the children have been badly taught in previous years. Some of them seem scarcely to have been taught at all. Undaunted, however, you confer with your teaching assistant, and resolve to arrange some remedial extra classes to fix the problem. Unknown to you, however – and remember you are still a newcomer to teaching – this scene is being replicated in classrooms up and down the land. Veteran teachers are of course expecting it, and have their plans already in place. But the question remains – why does this happen?

On occasion, the fault does lie with the standard of teaching itself, just as every sector has its failures. Schools in which this is the case are often marked by high staff turnover and excessive reliance on supply teachers (short-term agency staff, often called in at the last minute). When a child has multiple teachers in the same academic year, it's very easy for things to get lost in the gaps, and for children to lose their focus and motivation. Yet in most schools this is not the case: staffing levels are at least adequate, turnover is reasonable, teaching quality is generally fine. Nevertheless, almost every teacher will routinely encounter classes with some troubling gaps in their basic knowledge, with the exception of those secondary teachers fortunate enough to only teach the top sets.

My view is that the cause of this is not rampant teacher failure, but that teachers have been given a near-impossible task. The problem is usually not 'they were never taught'; the problem is the structure of the curriculum itself. It is simply too big, analogous to the bloated operating system we discussed in the first chapter. The effect of curriculum bloat is that children who struggle to master the basics often never quite do, because of the sheer pace with which their teachers have to take them through the curriculum. An overweight curriculum is the mortal enemy of classroom success. Children have an extraordinary capacity to forget things, and the lack of opportunity for frequent revision compounds the problem. There is nothing for it but some very radical curricular liposuction.

Let me illustrate the problem with some statistics. In a superb blog series investigating the problem of curricular bloat in the UK primary curriculum, Solomon Kingsnorth worked out that there are just 3.8 days for each Maths objective in the primary school syllabus. These objectives can be anything from 'read and write numbers up to 1000 in numerals and in words' in Year 3 to 'express missing number problems algebraically' in Year 6. The 3.8 days does not include the time needed for teacher training days, school trips, nativity rehearsals, sports days and so on.[1] Of course, you aren't teaching Maths all day, so in reality this leaves you with something more like 3 hours per learning objective, being generous.

At secondary level, the problem gets even worse. Kingsnorth has calculated that the number of objectives in the GCSE Maths curriculum is a full 203,[2] though he also notes that many of these objectives in fact contain multiple sub-objectives, such as 'order positive and negative integers, decimals and fractions', which obviously hides several different elements within one sentence. Nevertheless, sticking to the original tally, this works out to 1.9 teaching days per objective. This shrinks when you consider the realities of school life, so the reality is probably closer to more like an hour and twenty minutes (or less) per objective. Just as the curriculum gets more cognitively complex, and the concepts ever more difficult to master, we force children and teachers to march through at an even faster pace than we made them do in primary.

I decided to repeat this rather interesting exercise for the KS2 History curriculum, just out of curiosity. There are 39 weeks in the school year. If every primary school taught History for an hour a week, this would give us 156 hours of instructional time across KS2. In my experience this is a ludicrously optimistic assumption, given that History is normally sharing curriculum time with Geography and RE, so in reality I would guess that around 60 hours is a much more realistic estimate, and still probably too high.

In 60 hours, pupils are expected to learn the history of Britain all the way from the Stone Age up to the Norman Conquest. In addition, they are expected to be immersed in local study, and study a theme or aspect of British history that goes beyond 1066. In addition to that, they are required to conduct an in-depth study of the achievements of the earliest recorded civilizations (such as Ancient Egypt or the Chinese Shang Dynasty). In addition to that, they are also supposed to study Ancient Greek history and culture. In addition to that, they are required to study in detail one non-European society that provides a useful contrast with British history, such as Baghdad circa AD 900, or the Mayan civilization of around the same time. Unlike the Mayan calendar, the History curriculum seems to have no end.

Anyone who knows anything about small children and primary schools is well aware that at this point the national curriculum has become a charade. I would bet that there is not a single primary school in the country meeting the full set of expectations, statutory and non-statutory, in the History primary curriculum. Even if we restrict ourselves solely to the more minimalist statutory requirements, and be very generous when it comes to agreeing what counts as meeting them, I'm still not sure many schools would clear the bar.

How has this state of affairs come about? In part, I think, because politicians failed to understand just how squeezed the instructional time for the rest of the curriculum would become when primary schools have such a massive incentive to teach English and Maths above all else, since that is what they are held accountable for in exams. The objectives seem to have been constructed with a delusionally optimistic idea of the time available to teach them. What would be an ambitious but just-about-achievable curriculum for 156 hours of instructional time simply doesn't work at all when you realise that only a third as many hours are available.

Returning to you as our hypothetical newly qualified teacher – are you still brimming with optimism, now you know just how many hurdles have been put in front of you? Any readers who became teachers overnight as a result of the coronavirus lockdown will know how long it can take to embed new learning. While I think I managed to teach my youngest the 'bus stop' method of division in less than 3 hours, allowing him time to then practise it and for me to pick up misconceptions and then correct them and reinforce his knowledge simply isn't feasible in such a short time. And that's one child, not 30.

In part, the problem is also due to the natural process of bureaucratic bloat, where all sorts of special-interest groups have made sure to get their special area of interest into the curriculum. You can see this especially clearly in the primary History curriculum, which lists a set of suggested historical worthies, the lives of which pupils might study. You can almost see the painstaking care that went into this list. The compilers evidently didn't want to annoy the 'Great Men making Great Discoveries' traditionalist historians, so they included Christopher Columbus and Neil Armstrong; but they also clearly thought it vital to keep feminists on board, so Emily Davison is on the list as well. Likewise those who campaign for an ethnically inclusive curriculum also needed to be pleased, hence the inclusion of Mary Seacole and, oddly enough, Rosa Parks, whose inclusion might be thought very odd given how focused the rest of the curriculum is on British history. Given that Black History Month is October, it is quite plausible that the first history a British child encounters as they begin their schooling career is the historical politics of the civil rights movement in 1960s Alabama. This pattern is only set to continue, with the global social justice protests leading to calls to further revise the curriculum.

However it occurs, curriculum bloat ensures that what pupils actually learn bears little to no resemblance to the paper curriculum. This comes with costs. In many schools it ensures that learning is a mile wide and an inch deep. The problem is very bad for non-core subjects (what a depressing phrase) such as History, but is quite severe even for Maths and English. As discussed above, it ensures that gaps between children in their understanding only ever grow wider, since there is no time to ameliorate them. The less well you know something, the easier it is to forget. An overcrowded curriculum ensures that few children know many things well, and long summer holidays allow them plenty of time to forget.

A child's success in learning a new concept is heavily dependent on their prior knowledge. Neuroscientists tell us that prior knowledge acts as 'a structure into which the new information can be integrated'.[3] Research suggests that knowledge cannot simply be added to the brain in a slapdash fashion – 'memory performance' depends on how well this knowledge has been built upon pre-existing knowledge. Like any solid structure, a well-performing mind has to be built on solid foundations.

A child with shaky prior knowledge will, unfortunately, easily forget new concepts. To pick a very basic example, it is much harder to master long multiplication if you are shaky on your times tables, because while you are doing sums you have to think about two things at once: the way long multiplication works, and your times tables. Remember the example of the plumber fixing the toilet? If you have mastered the times tables, this frees up a great deal of working memory (through the cognitive load we discussed in chapter 3), and allows you to focus solely on getting comfortable with the algorithm. Likewise, it is much easier to think up an excellent piece of creative writing if you can devote all your attention to imaginative world-building and character creation, and aren't limited by constantly having to think about spelling and grammar.

Automaticity and brilliance are natural allies. Mastery is the best friend of innovation. By making it next to impossible for most children to master anything, we have excluded them from excellence. We greatly value innovation and creativity and we are rightly proud of our outstanding achievements in both technology and the arts. Yet curriculum bloat is choking innovation in our schools – both pedagogical innovation from teachers and creative responses from pupils.

In short, curriculum bloat has created a system that gives an overwhelming advantage to children with excellent memories (and those able to afford additional tutoring or independent schools with longer school days), and strongly punishes others. This is perhaps reflected in the fact that inequality of outcome is relatively high in England compared with other nations.[4] The raw magnitude of the gap is absolutely enormous: in PISA 2015, the top 10% of English 15-year-olds were the equivalent of *eight full academic years* in mathematics ahead of their peers in the bottom 10%. Even at younger ages, where the gaps are normally smaller, it is not at all uncommon to find children in primary classrooms who are about two years ahead across the board, *working in the same classroom* as children who are two years behind. The average Year 4 teacher, therefore, is quite often trying to teach children working at a Year 6 level as well as children working at a Year 2 level. Not only is this difficulty partly caused by curriculum bloat, but that issue makes it even harder to accommodate such cognitive diversity.

It is of course inevitable that some children will learn faster than others, especially as the curriculum becomes more cognitively complex as children age, but there are good reasons to think we could do somewhat better. At the moment, our solution is apparently to try to avoid thinking too hard about the sheer magnitude of the gap. At primary, we try to avoid giving standardised tests, and when we do, we give children and parents alike generally vague and imprecise feedback. At secondary level, we generally put children in different sets, which can be pedagogically useful, but also serves to avoid the awkward situation of having to confront the stark reality where the 15-year old with the mathematics ability of the average 10-year-old is in the same room with the one with capabilities matching the average 18-year old.

But teaching children in sets undoubtedly has a negative impact on the 'growth mindset' of the children put in the lower sets – the ability to understand that one's abilities and performance can be developed and improved, rather than being stuck in a certain place.[5] Teaching by ability rather than age does seem attractive, but I am also concerned about what this means socially for older pupils having to work with those two years (or more) their junior. Well-designed technology can play a role here as it can silently personalise content to a student's ability, without alerting their peers or socially ostracising them.

So, dear newly qualified teacher, a bad curriculum is a massive threat to your students' learning and development. But curriculum bloat also inhibits your expertise as a professional. The more prescribed content a teacher has to get through, the less time they have to enrich the lives of pupils with some more specialised but powerful knowledge of their own. The high-flying Oxbridge English graduate with a specialism in Anglo-Saxon literature might love to teach the children in their school about *Beowulf,* a poem they know a great deal about, but it is quite plausible they will simply have no time to do so, so numerous are the statutory boxes to be ticked. This has obvious implications for recruitment and retention. Our Oxbridge English graduate is far less likely to go into and stay in the teaching profession if they realise that disappointingly little of their rich, specialised expertise is actually useful in the classroom. No one wants to be a mere vehicle for delivering whatever content politicians and assorted special-interest groups have decided to cram into the curriculum. Furthermore, the less room schools have for manoeuvre, the less ability they have to customise the curriculum to their local context, which is especially important for humanities subjects.

This lack of options for customisation can be very extreme. At primary level, perhaps the most acute example is how the government has put together a list of words that they have decided all students must learn. Someone at the Department for Education actually thought it was a good idea to produce a list of specific words that teachers are compelled by statute to make sure their pupils can spell. That pupils should have good spelling is of course uncontroversial. That the government can or should decide for a teacher which words they specifically need to teach is simply silly. It simply disenfranchises teachers for no obviously good reason. Guidance is usually good, while prescription is usually bad.

Curriculum bloat affects the minds of teachers, as well as students. How easy is it to prioritise what children really need when you have a vast list of objectives to get through and only a couple of hours to teach each of them? It is so easy to get sucked into the miasma of 'things you have to do' that you lose sight of what you really ought to be doing, especially as an inexperienced teacher. What is the purpose in teaching a child long multiplication when they struggle with times tables and column addition? Yet an age-based structure of schooling coupled with a very prescriptive curriculum ensures that teachers struggle to personalise education for the children who need it most. Even if you, our hypothetical teacher friend from the opening of this chapter – no doubt an observant and clever individual – figure out exactly where the gaps are in your pupils' learning, how much spare time can you really expect to carve out to do anything about it?

Solutions to curriculum bloat

In response to this problem, many schools have become creative. In some institutions there are children who almost never attend assembly, since that time is all that's available to try to fill the gaps in their understanding. Other children find their time in non-core subjects such as music, drama or art dramatically limited. They sit uneasily on a treadmill of interventions, pull-out programmes and tutoring – all relentlessly focused on core subjects since high-stakes assessment ensures the narrowing of the curriculum, a problem that curriculum bloat compounds. This is all rather sad, but it is a logical response to an obvious problem. There are simply not enough hours in the school day to properly teach the curriculum in its present state to all but a small minority of children.

Many parents, of course, are alert to this issue. They also realise that the obvious solution is simply to extend the number of hours in the day beyond what is normal. The result is the growth of a vast shadow schooling market. Whether this takes the form of 'cram schools' (or *juku*, as the Japanese versions are known), or private tutoring (as is more customary in England), the popularity of shadow schooling should be understood largely not as a condemnation of the teachers who work in mainstream schools, but as a rational response to an overly demanding curriculum. As understandable as this may be, it seems rather unfortunate that the natural happiness of childhood is often so radically curtailed by the frequently dreary and repetitive business of education. The demise of 'children's culture' is surely not just due to video games, urbanisation and crime – which combined has resulted in children confined to their homes, and ended the era of children who ran wild. It is surely also a story of homework, shadow schooling, and the ever-growing encroachment of school into every facet of a child's life. To paraphrase Pink Floyd, curriculum – leave those kids alone.

Is there any viable solution on the horizon? Once again, Solomon Kingsnorth has presented some fascinating possibilities, some of them fictional, some of them real. In one superb thought experiment he posits a primary school in Cornwall that imports a Japanese headteacher and his 'Hitaisho' method.[6] School lunches would definitely get more interesting, but the point of this idea is a radical curricular simplification. Reception has just two objectives: all children can count to 20 and back, and all children know the alphabet perfectly. All teaching time is devoted to these objectives alone; the rest is given over to storytelling and play. In Year 1, there are just three objectives for the entire year: mastering a list of phonemes and graphemes (smaller units of speaking and writing), fluent counting to 110 and back, and perfect memorisation of all number bonds to 20. All non-teaching time is once again devoted to storytelling, play, poems, songs, and every form of oral language development imaginable, all mediated through a never-ceasing flow of fairy-tales. Writing is gone, sent up the curriculum to the higher years, once all children are fluent readers. The outcome is superb results in Year 6, due to the time taken to get the basics right, and the imagination that is cultivated through vast exposure to rich vocabulary and beautiful stories.

The school is fictional, as is the Hitaisho method, though it does bear resemblance to elements of real-life practice in Japan. Nevertheless, there are some places in the real world we could perhaps learn from, some closer to home than Japan. Kingsnorth points to Estonia, a relatively poor European nation that nevertheless performs extremely well in PISA.[7] Not only do schools in Estonia enjoy a very high level of local autonomy, but the national curriculum is significantly shorter and more straightforward than its British equivalent. Kingsnorth calculates that the GCSE-equivalent Maths curriculum is 83% smaller than the UK version, allowing 10 hours of instructional time per objective, which contrasts very favourably with time permitted per objective here (little more than an hour). He also analyses the Maths curriculum for ages 7 to 12 (the equivalents of Year 2 to Year 6 in England, since school starting age in Estonia is higher) and finds that at this age the curriculum allows an average of 23 days per objective, as contrasted with just 3.8 days (in reality fewer) in England.

This evidence is of course merely suggestive, and we have no strong reason to draw a link between Estonia's more stripped-down curriculum and its very impressive educational performance. It is perfectly possible that other factors are responsible, though teaching is not especially well paid (and, historically, was very badly paid), nor is it uniquely high status in the way that it is in other high-performing European countries, such as Finland. Academic qualifications-wise, Estonian teachers are much more like those in the UK and the US. In turn, this makes it more likely that the curriculum could be a contributory factor, though no doubt Estonia benefits substantially from the 'small country effect' that seems to be a common occurrence in international comparisons, which sees countries like Estonia, Finland and Vietnam outperform many far larger and richer nations.

Nevertheless, the question certainly merits further investigation. I am always somewhat sceptical about drawing lessons for big countries from the high performance of very small ones, but we should consider trialing a pared-back curriculum in England, implemented with plenty of local autonomy (something on which Estonia also ranks highly in PISA's data). Surely a free school or academy trust could be set up that used its freedom to model its curriculum on the Estonian approach?

Even if we nail the size of the curriculum, you still have to decide what content it actually includes. You could have a radically reduced curriculum that is still totally useless because the objectives themselves are suboptimal, or even harmful. At this point the great knowledge vs skills debate rears its head once again. Should the curriculum be largely a body of knowledge that students must learn, or describe a set of skills for students to acquire? Is the optimal approach the English model of a knowledge-based national curriculum, or something more like the Scottish 'Curriculum for Excellence', which focuses more on skills? It is worth praising the increasingly popular International Baccalaureate. Once the darling of high-flying diplomats and businessmen, the IB's focus on both academic rigour and non-curricular skills has seen it spread into schools of all types across the world.[8]

I must confess to a certain impatience with the endless debate over knowledge versus skills, since in reality you cannot have skills without knowledge, and vice versa. The question 'which is more valuable' is a false one. While in theory employers might say they value flexible skills above all, every useful skill is dependent on underlying knowledge. The skill to write excellent fiction is dependent upon a broad knowledge of the genre and knowing a wide range of plots, stories, legends and common character archetypes. No non-fiction writer starts a book with a tabula rasa, at least not if the book is going to be any good: they will bring a swathe of pre-existing knowledge, which will then be deepened during the research process. Is the ability to research something independently a skill? Of course, but again it's based on knowledge, such as knowing what the best reliable sources for the domain are, and where to access them.

When designing a curriculum, it is more than possible to combine both knowledge and skills, such as immersing children in a world of complex and rich literary texts that contain many layers of meaning, so that children learn the skills of inference as the natural product of knowledge, not as an isolated set of techniques.

But time is still limited, and this leaves us still having to choose between Beowulf, Chaucer and the poems of Carol Ann Duffy, for example. Which shall we choose, and why? Discussions of this kind quickly stagnate into an irresolvable mire. Just about the only thing that people agree on is a good deal of Shakespeare, but even then there is huge debate over interpretations.

The job of curriculum construction is about making trade-offs: we will focus on *this*, teach it properly and in depth, but regrettably that means we will not have time for *that*. You might think that the 'Hitaisho' method of just two objectives for an entire year in Reception – and only three for Year 1 – takes things a bit too far. It probably does. But if this chapter has communicated one thing, it should be that there are no free lunches, and every addition to the curriculum achieves greater breadth at the cost of some depth.

In chapter 3, I discussed certain skills that I think are missing from the modern curriculum, such as teamwork, autodidactism and adaptability. This might sound like prescription, an act of hypocrisy given everything I have just said. But the curriculum can be enriched as I recommend without the addition of yet more prescription. If we wish to promote these key skills in schools, we would do better to liberate teachers from the current stranglehold of curricular prescription than to simply add some vague verbiage about 'ensuring all children are self-directed learners' 50,000 words deep into the national curriculum, where it will be duly forgotten about.

A radically stripped-down curriculum would allow far more time for teachers to use their natural creativity. This natural creativity is one of the great assets of the teacher workforce; the job naturally attracts great communicators, lovers of the arts, craftsmen and craftswomen – and we squander their talents ruthlessly. Are there any teachers out there that don't want their pupils to emerge with superb creative skills, and wouldn't autonomously work towards that goal if given half a chance? I doubt it.

Let me add a note of caution. The curriculum problem cannot be solved in isolation. The best curriculum in the world could still be useless in a world of high-stakes accountability where the tests are poorly aligned to the curriculum, because under high-stakes accountability people teach to the test. We have to solve the many problems with the way we test pupils and hold schools to account, otherwise any improved curriculum will be not worth the pdf it's written on.

Chapter 7: We treasure what we measure

'Not everything that can be counted counts, and not everything that counts can be counted.'
William Bruce Cameron

Do you remember the quadratic formula? How confident are you with long division? How about trigonometry? What is an atom called when it gains or loses electrons? What piece of punctuation is employed when a noun phrase is used to qualify another noun? The answer incidentally is a hyphen, as in 'stainless-steel knife'. Presumably you once did know most of these things from GCSE or O-levels, and many teachers reading this book will still know them, because they teach this material regularly. For the average person, however – most definitely including myself – it's quite a different story.

We spend enormous amounts of time teaching pupils to memorise material like this, which they then promptly forget. We do so purely so they can pass high-stakes exams, many of which are more important for the government than the pupils. What we teach, and the way in which we do so, is increasingly driven not by rational decisions but the demands of the high-stakes testing system. The tail is not merely wagging the dog, but is wrapping itself around his throat and strangling him to death. Under the pressure, teachers suffer, and it harms their pupils' development.

School assessment, in a sane world, should achieve four main goals, which we will come on to. These goals can be met simply, cheaply, and in the same format at the same time. The word 'assessment' brings to mind A levels, GCSEs, SATs, the times tables check, the phonics screening check, as well as a whole host of unloved and now abolished national tests such as Key Stage 3 SATs. Just writing all these in one sentence makes my chest tighten – the stress! But it doesn't have to be this way, and definitely shouldn't be.

It's as true in assessment as it is with everything else – we treasure what we measure. This flows from the top, from international bodies right down to teachers. This is the reason why emphasis on measures like the EBacc – the English accountability measure that holds schools to account for pupils' performance in five core academic subjects – is a problem. This squeezes out the arts, sports, design and more – the very subjects in which the vital 'soft skills' previously discussed are most learned. Many of us learned the importance of teamwork the second we set foot on the hockey pitch or the rugby field, or actually just before, during a strategy session in the changing rooms. We learned leadership as captain of the rounders team or at the Model United Nations, and we learned the value of hard work by practising instruments and languages.

But before we get bogged down in the mud of assessment, we should first ask what it is we want to achieve. Again, sadly, this is the subject of intense ideological debate. But there exists common ground that most sensible people would agree on. Firstly, assessment helps teachers to know their pupils' performance and gaps in learning, informing their teaching. Secondly, it's quite clear that students need to leave formal education with some sort of 'asset' proving they have gained a certain level of knowledge and skills so they can go on to further education, higher education, an apprenticeship or whatever they desire. Thirdly, we need to be able to have some sense of how schools are performing, both to shine a light on what works and also to ensure that children aren't being let down. Finally – and this is probably the most contentious – it is potentially helpful to conduct international comparisons in order to measure the success of government-level education reforms.

Goal 1: Helping teachers to teach better

On one level, very simply put, assessment should inform the teacher what their pupils have learned, and where the gaps are. Assessment allows teachers to spot patterns of mistakes. It is one thing to know that Jimmy struggles with long multiplication, it is quite another to know that this happens because he's getting the numbers muddled up when doing the addition at the end. Assessment transforms a vague objective ('Jimmy needs to learn to write in a more interesting way') to something concrete and specific that can be actioned ('Jimmy needs to scale up his vocabulary with more terms that are appropriate for academic writing, and vary his sentence structure every now and then').

Assessment for this purpose can be done in a very low-stakes, informal way. Teachers do it all the time when they mark classwork or homework – though this marking creates its own problems when it comes to teacher workload (but more on this later). There is no need to conduct national examinations just for teachers to find out what their pupils have learned, and arguably doing so is actually counterproductive, since it incentivises 'cram and forget'. Assessment is absolutely vital to get right, since it is one of the most powerful devices in a teacher's toolkit, as well as something that can easily make their lives miserable when done poorly.

Assessment as a pedagogical tool is inextricably tied in with feedback. Without assessment there is less to give feedback on. Without feedback the pupil's ability to improve their own performance is naturally very limited. But for the feedback to be meaningful, the assessment has to be both reliable and valid. In layman's terms, this simply means that the assessment has to be an accurate measure of the pupil's true level of performance. This is much more complicated than it sounds, especially as the learning domain broadens. Learning is invisible and hence very hard to assess.

A simple example will suffice here. Let's say we asked a child what year the Battle of Hastings happened, and they didn't know. It would seem reasonable to draw the inference that the child knows very little about the Norman Conquest. What if, however, we asked some more questions, and it turns out the child knows the battle was fought between the Saxon army of Harold and the Norman forces of William the Conqueror, Harold was probably killed with an arrow to the eye, and the battle led to the Norman takeover of the English aristocracy? Now our inference has quite radically changed. It seems that, after all, the child knows quite a lot about the Norman Conquest, and for some reason they just happened to forget the date of the battle.

In a nutshell, this is the sampling problem. What we want to assess is very extensive, and for practical reasons we can normally only question a pupil on a very small portion of it. The key, therefore, is to assess the pupil on just enough questions to capture their knowledge of the broader domain. It is not sufficient to ask only one question about the Battle of Hastings if you want to get a good idea of what the pupil knows about the Norman Conquest: you need to ask perhaps six or seven.

Something similar is true even in domains that seem ostensibly narrower, such as basic mathematics. Take long multiplication for example. When assessing a child on long multiplication, you are also assessing them on their fluency in times tables, their ability to do column addition, and their ability to remember how to multiply by tens as well as units. Furthermore, you are assessing their ability to do all of this accurately. If you only set the pupil a couple of long multiplication questions, and they get one or both of them wrong – does this tell you anything meaningful about their true level of understanding? Not necessarily. It might well be that they just so happened to make a silly mistake, and if you set them another 30 similar questions, they would get most of them right.

Goal 2: Assets for students

The main point of end-of-school exams – the useful reason as to why they actually exist – is as a summary metric that signals to employers 'by the end of this child's school career they have at a bare minimum learned this much'. It is convenient to have a summary metric, an end-of-school test, since compiling all the in-school data on a particular pupil for employers or higher education institutions to review is simply not practical (yet this will change radically given the pace of technological innovation).

Once again, however, although national examinations currently serve this purpose better than any other solution that is in widespread use, they don't do so very well. Grade inflation is part of the reason why.

Just as one problem with high inflation in the financial sphere is that it makes price discovery quite difficult, so too high grade inflation makes ability discovery very difficult. What does this mean? Simply put, if too many children are getting A grades, then employers and universities have no way of knowing which children just barely scraped the grade with loads of help from their parents, tutors and teachers, and which of them breezed through with no trouble at all. This was precisely the reason that the A* grade was invented, first for GCSEs and later for A levels – to allow for meaningful ability discovery, wherein the highest achievers could genuinely distinguish themselves.

Even without grade inflation, teaching to the test, cheating and all the other problems that lower the validity of high-stakes national examinations, there is a more fundamental problem with such tests as signals of ability. Just because a child can do something at a single point in time, after at least two years of hard work, that doesn't mean they can perform that same task at a later date. This is the 'cram and forget' problem.

This is not an insurmountable issue for employers, because while it does mean that the average adult is probably rather less academically knowledgeable than their test scores would imply, at the very least if you knew something at point X in your life, you presumably have the capability to learn it again with a bit of revision later on. Employers, furthermore, are not necessarily looking for the ability to learn trigonometry specifically, but to learn fairly complex mathematical and statistical skills more broadly as part of the on-the-job training – the underlying ability to learn being more valuable than the actual specific skill of mastering trigonometry. It is very questionable, however, whether large-scale national examinations are the best way of actually measuring this ability.

But 'cram and forget' permanently damages how students view learning. This is summarised by the late sociology professor Peter Kaufman's description of his experience of teaching students fresh from high school: 'Too often, the students just want to be told what they need to learn to pass the test or what they need to write to get a good grade on a paper.'[1] Their experience of the school exam system means they forgot how to be the 'self-directed and genuine learners that they were when they first entered school'.

Goal 3: Accountability

Standardised tests, where all pupils answer the same questions and receive the same scores relative to their performance, are used by governments to hold schools to account for the standard of education offered to their students. The results are also used by parents when deciding on schools for their children. But given everything we know about the perils of our exam system, is this a good idea? Is our intense focus on a narrow set of results encouraging schools to be less accountable for the education they provide and instead nudging them to focus on what amounts to a very small aspect of a child's development?

Rightfully, schools are being increasingly held to account for the progress their pupils make at school, rather than just raw numbers of how many students reached a certain arbitrary level. In England, the 'Progress 8' system attempts to measure how well children progress between the end of primary school and the end of secondary. Introduced in 2016, Progress 8 measures pupils' performance in eight key subjects and schools are given a score based on the average of these. No more focusing all one's efforts on getting every child over a grade boundary, and the hard work of the lowest-achieving students is as rewarded as the hard work of those already near the top. At least in theory.

But Progress 8 is not a perfect measure by anyone's standards. Educationalist Daisy Christodoulou points out that the system cannot reliably be used to measure the performance of ability-selected classes, as schools frequently move pupils between sets based on their recent progress. Classes split between 'recent attainment and work ethic', as is often the case, makes the measure redundant for measuring the performance of many classes.[2] This is because the top set often ends up being the class of the fastest progressing pupils, muddying the waters.

The measure also completely ignores the background of pupils – something that headteachers consistently tell me is one of the biggest problems with the accountability system. Bristol University found that London's great Progress 8 score 'more than halves' when results are adjusted to consider pupil background, primarily because these schools teach many 'high progress ethnic groups'.[3] Similarly, the North East of England's low score 'increases substantially' when adjusting for the high prevalence of poverty in the area. The high performance of grammar schools and faith schools is slashed when the 'advantaged nature of their pupils is considered'. I am cautious of reaffirming the 'soft bigotry of low expectations', but the weight of the calls from headteachers suggests that pupil background should be a factor.

When first introduced, the measure was so badly designed that the ratings could be 'distorted by poor performance from a handful of pupils', such as those entering no exams.[4] The government was forced to redesign the system to exclude these 'outliers', choosing to then publish two different versions of the measure every year. It's no surprise that leading headteacher Stephen Tierney said the new system would 'probably confuse more people that it helps'.[5]

Like all measurements, Progress 8 influenced the actions of those being measured. Researchers from King's College London noted that the new system will force schools to focus less on more able students and more on the less able. Progress 8 'will require schools radically to rethink their policies on teaching and learning', the study said.[6] This is not necessarily a bad outcome, and it is not my intention to judge either way. But Progress 8 highlights how the accountability system should not be dictating the policies of headteachers and teachers, who know far better how to educate their unique groups of learners than an inanimate measure cooked up by the government ever could.

Goal 4: International comparisons

If you thought exams designed to compare a country's schools sound unworkable, how on earth could exams ever hope to be used to compare countries as different as Luxembourg and Vietnam? Since 2000, the OECD has attempted to measure the performance of countries across the world in maths, science and reading. Its PISA tests are sat by 15 year olds every three years and are designed to shine a light on education policy best practice. The theory is that as the data begins to pile up, governments will be able to make informed, evidence-based decisions about how to design their education systems.

In practice, the PISA tests have – *quelle surprise* – not been universally well received. Institute of Education professor Stephen Ball described the 'tremendously distorting effect' of the tests, suggesting that the focus of education policy across the world has been diverted towards improving PISA scores.[7] What began as an honest attempt to boost evidence-based policy-making has become a pseudoscientific vanity metric, with data being cherry-picked by politicians to justify their preferred outcomes. Do you want to ban technology from schools? Simply find a country that doesn't use much technology, and hail their great results. Do you want to give every child an iPad? There's a country for that too.

Some countries are beginning to tire of PISA. Luxembourg is reducing its participation in the tests, with its Education Minister suggesting the country's low scores are irrelevant as its pupils are tested 'in a language that is not their mother tongue', it is the only country to have 'more than 50% of 15 year olds with a migratory background' and it is the only country to have a completely trilingual education system.[8] India pulled out for a decade, citing concerns that the tests wouldn't consider differences of background, class or caste among its pupils.[9] These aren't valid excuses for poor performance on tests, but that's not the point – the point is that it is not possible to design a test that will fairly take the unique circumstances of almost 80 different countries into account.

Mission creep also saw the OECD introduce additional tests that will 'assess [pupils'] respect for other cultures, challenge extremism and help identify fake news'. These are valid concerns, but hardly the job of an international testing body. England and the US decided that this was not good use of schools' time, and pulled out of these extra tests.[10]

On the flipside, however imperfect, the rankings do serve a purpose of holding failing education ministries to account. Scottish politicians mulled pulling out of the PISA tests in 2010, auguring the country's worst ever performance in the 2016 tests.[11] The results piled pressure on the Scottish government to improve its schools, suggesting the tests can provide a much-needed punt to the posterior. The tests enable an imperfect yet useful way to compare countries' performance and have been described as 'the premier resource to measure the divergence of education systems'.[12] Yet this leads to the bizarre situation where every three years a new darling education system appears, sending educationalists and politicians panicking to copy every aspect of the winner's school system in the hope of repeating their success.

Finland, once considered the pinnacle of educational excellence, has fallen in the tests every year since 2006, while the 'gaps between rich and poor pupils are widening'.[13] Finnish success in the early PISA tests 'spurned many of the market and accountability reforms undertaken' across the world.[14] The problem is that there is about as much causal evidence that Finnish success was caused by certain aspects of its schooling structure as it was caused by the Finnish taste for reindeer. London School of Economics researcher Gabriel Heller Sahlgren argues that Finland's educational rise precedes its shift to low accountability and high autonomy, and that until the 1990s, 'the Finnish education system was centralised and had little autonomy'.[15] The paper suggests that Finland's more recent fall may be due to more traditional teaching methods being replaced by the pupil-led reforms that have drawn international praise. Sahlgren also suggests that the high status of Finnish teachers stems from how teachers played a vital role in the development of Finnish nationhood in the face of Russian rule in the 19th century, rather than any modern reforms that could be copied by other nations.

As Patrik Scheinin, Professor of Education at the University of Helsinki, puts it, 'we do a lot of strange things like taking off our shoes [at school], or having a lot of reindeer per capita, and other things that are specific to Finland but have probably nothing to do with any PISA explanation'.[16]

So what do we do?

Already we can see that the process of conducting meaningful assessment is much more complicated than it might appear to be. I'm not here to set out a perfectly designed assessment and accountability system, mostly because such a thing will likely never exist. But having considered the failures of our existing approach, there are a number of concrete improvements we can make.

The most fundamental improvement that could be made would be to shift away from summative to formative assessment. This can be done without totally abandoning end-of-year exams – they instead become part of a wider, formative package. The wild end-of-year celebrations would remain – but the dreaded summative exam would lose its dread, becoming only a small part of the child's outcome. As we previously discussed, formative assessment is based on regular low-stakes tests that teachers give to understand their pupils' progress. These could be used as a measure of accountability in schools. They are far less stressful for teachers and pupils, and regular data is far more reliable and accurate.

Regarding providing students with an asset of some sort, we must shift towards a system based on promoting lifelong learning. Education does not end at 16 or 18 or even in your 20s. Here is where technology can help. Most people have a LinkedIn profile – but imagine a more advanced type of digital credential passport that consisted of more than simply nauseating corporate banter and spam from salespeople and recruiters. Imagine a digital passport, or portfolio, with minute detail of your educational and professional achievements, based on data from your time in school and credentials issued by educational and professional establishments. This would provide you with a way of displaying to employers how you really shine as an individual, using data far more sophisticated and bespoke than just 'I've got a degree in History from Leeds University and I enjoy teamwork'. Rather than relying on the very small amount of data produced by end-of-year exams, a digital passport could use formative assessment data, metacognitive testing data, and data on work completed throughout your educational career. This is entirely possible and at CENTURY we have developed such a system in response to younger students wanting a more holistic digital passport and one which they can continuously improve.

This begs the question of how we regulate qualifications. If any qualification can be delivered, such as the increasing number of micro-degrees available online, how can we ensure quality? Ofqual, the regulator of qualifications, serves this function for school qualifications in the UK, but we now have marketplace technologies – platforms which match students with online nano-degrees (shorter online degrees which are often project and skills based). A student plugs in their goals, circumstances and experience, and an algorithm suggests the nano-degree most suitable to their individual needs. The test of whether they can use the knowledge they have sought and apply it will be for the employer to judge. We must let a thousand flowers bloom – employers will soon be able to judge which qualifications are truly valuable. This will democratise education and help to level the playing field. Opening up access to education and being able to display one's achievements with a digital passport will help people across the board and increase social mobility.

Our assessment system should not be about catching people out. GCSEs should not be the equivalent of a speed camera van hiding in a lay-by. It should be a positive system of improvement – for students, teachers and those who design the education system. Students need to have a record of achievement, but this can be provided in other ways without one set of high-stakes tests. These simply stress everyone out, from the pupils and their parents to the teachers and their heads. It doesn't benefit anyone. Smaller tests that produce micro-credentials that allow learners to continuously improve will particularly benefit late bloomers and those who begin or change their careers later in life. There is a risk that frequent smaller tests could be stressful – but in reality, these 'tests' can be no more strenuous than the light-touch checks that teachers already do on their students week in, week out.

Shorter, frequent tests also better allow us to self-correct when we are going wrong. Micro-credentials allow us to take different routes to upskill ourselves in many areas, whereas longer courses tie you down for three years – acceptable for certain professions such as medicine or law, but too much of a commitment for many seeking roles in fields such as business, marketing or technology.

Standardised tests have got a terrible reputation over the years, but in reality this is purely because they are so often used for the purposes of high-stakes accountability, with all the inherent problems therein. Standardised tests do not need to be high-stakes tests. Most everyday tests taken in the classroom by the same group of students, at the same time, under the same conditions and marked with the same marking scheme are standardised tests. Divorced from the context of high-stakes accountability, standardised tests are actually a powerful tool for teaching and learning. Done in a formative way, children benefit and understand that the tests are part of continuous learning in which they can always improve, rather than a permanent stamp on their forehead.

Assessment and accountability are two of the toughest educational nuts to crack. The suggestions above will help – but any top-down reforms imposed on schools will be doomed to fail at worst, or further tie teachers' hands at best. As discussed previously, we must return to valuing teachers as expert professionals who are more than capable of teaching and nurturing young people without constant interference from those outside the profession.

Chapter 8: The Village

'It takes a village to raise a child.'
Proverb

We've looked at where education is going wrong and how we might begin to fix it. But a school provides far more than the transfer of information from a textbook to a child's brain. It's even far more than learning and discovery.

Despite its disputed origins, the above proverb accurately depicts how schools play a role far more diverse than just educating children. At school, children are provided with socialisation; their mental health is strengthened by their interactions with adults and fellow children; their teachers act as role models; and they are given fresh meals, refuge from any issues at home, and the opportunity to build lifelong memories and friendships.

English children are required to spend roughly 900 hours in a classroom every year.[1] Other countries range from around 600 to 1200 hours – but even at the lower end, this is a serious proportion of one's life spent within the school gates. These hours don't include breaks or any other time not spent on learning. Even so, time formally devoted to classroom learning offers far more to the child than just the acquisition of knowledge and skills. A child's interaction with a teacher is different from that with their parents – they are by their nature less intimate and more formal, which itself demands of children the development of maturity and self-reliance. School is where we mostly learn these vital traits, as well as the characteristics that allow us to flourish in later life – most importantly learning how to operate in a pro-social and cooperative manner with others towards shared group goals.

The world that children enter after leaving school is changing at a rapid pace. So fast, it seems, that we often lose sight of what really matters, to the point where children are now leaving the education system increasingly unprepared for life. One of the most important educational problems won't be found in a classroom, on a whiteboard or even in the Department for Education – it is far closer to home, and no teacher, student or parent is spared from its effects.

The mental health crisis

Let's talk about mental health.

There's little doubt that child and adolescent mental health has worsened over the last few years. The NHS-funded Mental Health of Children and Young People Survey is a data series that uses face-to-face interviews with a stratified random probability sample of children and their parents.[2] The results, for 5 to 15 year olds, show that the prevalence of mental health disorders in both young boys and girls has risen steadily in the last 20 years.

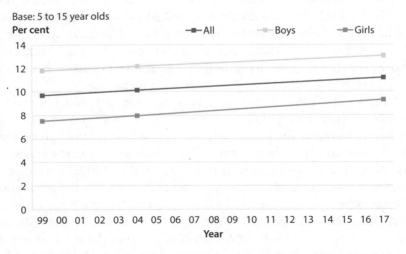

Prevalence of mental health disorders in 5 to 15 year olds (1999, 2004 and 2017)

A closer look at the data reveals that this trend is driven almost entirely by changes among 11 to 15 year olds. When you add additional data for 16 to 19 year olds, the extent of the crisis becomes increasingly clear.

Base: 5 to 19 year olds
Per cent

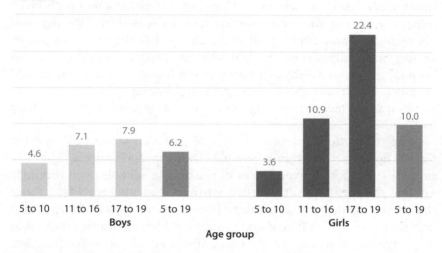

Prevalence of mental health disorders split into age groups (2017)

There are two obvious things that really jump out here: surprisingly high rates of mental distress in young boys (1 in 8 boys between ages 5 and 10 meeting the criteria for any diagnosable disorder, double the rate in girls), and incredibly high rates of mental distress in girls between 17 to 19 (almost 1 in 4 meeting the criteria for any diagnosable disorder).

Despite the data coming from an impeccable source (the NHS), skeptics are likely to challenge these findings and seek to explain them away, for example, by questioning the methodology of the study or putting them down to wider changing social patterns. They suggest that what people report or psychiatrists evaluate as a mental disorder today might have been thought of very differently in the past, with no actual change in the level of mental distress. Perhaps what once we called sadness, grief or nervousness is now diagnosed as a mental illness – but really people are much the same as they ever were. These may be valid concerns. However, these results cannot be simply put down to an increase in self-reporting because, sadly, there is considerable cross-validation available from other sources. Antidepressant prescriptions to children doubled in the UK between 2006 and 2015, with much of the increase among the 15 to 17 age group.[3] Hospital admissions for girls self-harming also doubled between 1997 and 2017, with girls three times more likely to self-harm than boys.[4] Suicide among children remains rare, but adolescent suicide rates increased by 7.9% per year between 2010 and 2017.[5] If all that's changed is the way that people answer and analyse surveys, then why do objective measures such as hospital admissions also show a rise? Nor is it obvious why there should be much bigger changes in how girls and young women respond to surveys, while men and young boys continue to answer much as they had before.

The straightforward and logical interpretation is that the reported figures do in fact indicate a genuine rise in mental distress. The data support the reported experiences of teachers in schools, who routinely say that the mental health burden on their students seems far greater than in days gone by, and that there is much more demand for specialist help such as CAMHS (Child and Adolescent Mental Health Services). A very large survey by the charity YoungMinds found that 94% of teachers who had been in the profession for more than five years felt that pupil mental health was deteriorating.[6] A poll by TeacherTapp found that 52% of teachers had raised concerns with a senior leader about the mental health of one or more of their pupils *in one month alone.*[7]

Perhaps the most curious thing about it all is that by most metrics, children are both objectively better off than they were: rates of teenage pregnancy, drug-taking and drinking are all hugely lower than they were a decade or two ago;[8] the number of children expecting to take A levels and study at university are up; and arrests of under-18s are down by three quarters over the last ten years (partly down to declining police capacity as their budgets have been cut, but also a genuine decline in child criminality).[9] If you look at the data one way, it appears that the current crop of children ought to be unusually happy and well adjusted, on course to become flourishing, productive members of society. Instead we find that children are much more miserable. They are simultaneously much worse off on one set of metrics and much better on another.

What on earth is going on? I'd love to be able to present a short, snappy answer, but there are probably a lot of different factors at work. Children in Britain and America are obviously under-exercised, overfed and growing up in increasingly unstable families as marriage rates decline: Britain in particular stands out among the OECD countries for its high family breakdown rate. Just 68% of children aged 0 to 14 live with both of their biological parents, compared to 95% in Finland.[10] Christian Guy of the Centre for Social Justice think tank said these figures highlight the 'forgotten families' in Britain – and forgotten families means forgotten, lost children.[11] Teenage girls in particular encounter a world where old rites of passage like dating are becoming endangered. The initiation into the adult world of love and romance is increasingly brutal, and sadly there isn't really any 'it gets better', as adult dating itself increasingly consists of numerous trivial encounters arranged on apps.

On top of this, it is becoming clear that the heavy use of social media is inimical to a healthy childhood. Where communication once took place at a human scale, face to face, it is now impersonal and over large distances, separating us from each other's emotions. Most teenagers say they prefer to talk to their friends online rather than in person, with texting overtaking talking in person in just a few years.[12] Most of these teens say they like doing things this way – but we have a responsibility to address the problems it is storing up. Communicating through a small screen, disconnected from other humans, used to be the reserve of dystopian novels. Detaching children from the consequences of their actions has resulted in many of them becoming downright nasty. Surveys suggest that a majority of teens have experienced cyberbullying, ranging from name-calling to having explicit images of them shared.[13] Unlike the face-to-face bullying of as recently as just a decade ago, it's harder to stand up to cyberbullies, it's harder to leave it at the school gates and it's harder to know who the bully is. Aside from its pernicious effect on mental health, research suggests the misuse of social media also harms academic performance.[14]

Whatever the cause of our mental health crisis, the effects are self-evident. But our collective response is inadequate. A 2017 UK government paper aimed to expand the number of designated mental health leads in schools and 'decide on the most effective way' to deliver Personal, Social and Health education, as well as Relationships and Sexual Education.[15] It promised to convene to look at the most effective way to keep children safe online. Mental Health Support Teams, linked to schools and partly managed by them, would be available to provide extra support for children with mild to moderate problems. Extra funding would allow for trials to access specialist NHS children's services with a four-week turnaround. The effects of these promises will not be felt for a few years yet – but it is clear that this is not exactly a groundbreaking rethink of the way we raise and nurture our children.

Within the media and within schools themselves, increasing attention is being placed on the mental health effects of school itself, particularly the impact of exams. Every headteacher I have spoken to has said exams create massive stress for both students and teachers, despite some educationalists dismissing these concerns. The competition to get into certain universities or secure jobs in the future is fierce. My discussion of the future of work in chapter 3 touched upon this – but to repeat, the loss of a 'job for life' or even a 'career for life' has serious mental health implications.

Young people are increasingly entering a world of work in which predictable, safe career paths are much less obvious than they were before. There's much more pressure to stay in education and complete qualifications than before, which means those students who do not enjoy schooling know they're going to be stuck with it for a good deal longer. The staples of adulthood – a stable job and home ownership – seem much more distant and unattainable, pushed over the horizon by ever-rising house prices and an educational process that quickly inflates in terms of both cost and length.

Perhaps it's not entirely surprising to learn that an OECD study found that British 15 year olds have unusually low levels of life satisfaction by international standards. Our teenagers reported the biggest decline in life satisfaction than any other country surveyed.[16] Britain was found to be the only country in Europe in which more than half of its children reported being regularly sad. Only children from a handful of nations, such as Taiwan and Japan, seem more lost and unsure of their purpose in the world than children from the UK. It is striking how American children do better on this score, comfortably above the OECD average;

not something you would obviously predict given the close transatlantic economic and cultural affinities. Perhaps America retains a greater sense of national narrative, with its global position providing a sense of purpose lacking in countries declining in their influence, like Britain. Or perhaps it's the influence of religion and community participation, both still much stronger features of American children's lives than is the case for their British counterparts.

Regardless, when the data point to such widespread cultural dysfunction, it hardly seems adequate that our collective response, from both within government and outside of it, is to expect schools to do even more with less money.

Some of the fault may lie with how the education system is structured, which I have addressed in previous chapters. Perhaps part of the reason children feel so worried about SATs and GCSEs is that they pick up on how stressed their teachers are about these exams. It doesn't make much logical sense for 11 year olds to be worried about their SATs, since the exams have little consequence for them. But it absolutely makes sense for their teachers to be worried, due to how the accountability system works. I could very easily believe that children, being perceptive creatures, respond to the worry and stress unconsciously emanating from one of the most important adult authority figures in their lives.

Improving our students' mental health

One argument is that children should be given lessons on 'grit' and 'resilience' – implying that we've just become a bit soft and that a few lessons in physical robustness would help stop young people slipping into depression. That's actually a real example; in 2015, the UK government paid for rugby coaches to go into English schools to try to toughen the kids up a bit, as part of a wider drive to instil grit and resilience in pupils. Nicky Morgan, the Education Secretary at the time, said that 'rugby teaches how to bounce back from setbacks, to show integrity in victory and defeat, and to respect others, especially your opponents'.[17] All of this is undoubtedly true. But is this the move of a government that is confident it has a solid plan in place to comprehensively tackle the mental health crisis that is sweeping the country? I'm not convinced –

and neither were schools, seeing as we've barely heard a peep about the scheme since it was announced.

With school budgets tightening, teachers themselves have been increasingly expected to improve their pupils' mental health, alongside teaching them and nurturing their development. However, each initiative that gives more responsibility to schools means more paperwork and meetings for teachers, more workload issues, and more risk of burnout. It represents another step of taking teachers away from their core mission of teaching. Putting so much social work and healthcare in schools is not cost-free: there is a real and finite cap on teacher time and mental space to tackle problems. If we want our teachers to be at their best, teaching the best lessons they can, happily and confidently, we need to resource schools adequately with the relevant professional expertise. We need both a short and long-term plan to improve our pupils' mental health.

The worst possible conclusion would be to assume that teachers will be able to solve the mental health crisis if we just bolt on a few extras to school provision and tweet a few more ostentatiously virtuous hashtags. Of course awareness helps, but unless this is matched with a real increase in resources, then we are doomed to fail.

While teachers play a vital role in spotting and reporting health issues facing their students, shifting the onus onto them will make the problem worse, while simultaneously reducing their ability to teach. Every single teacher wants nothing but the best for the children in their care. But the same can be said of every single doctor – yet we would never expect a GP to focus on improving their young patients' maths if they noticed they couldn't add something up in a consultation.

Having said that, schools are well-placed to monitor and feedback on child and adolescent mental health and even serve as part of the solution. Children spend almost 8000 hours at school over the course of their educational careers.[18] If we funded schools properly, with more specialist mental health staff, we could begin to turn the tide against the wave of mental health crises. The world is changing and our social environments are becoming less conducive to positive mental health. This means that mental health must become an urgent priority. At the moment schools do what they can, but when all they can afford to do is take half an hour out of a day for a chat about wellbeing or appoint a governor who understands the issue, then our economic priorities simply have to change.

This will cost a significant amount of money, but will be a lot less costly than the mental health bill the NHS will have to pay if we focus on cure rather than prevention. If we don't act, we will also have to continue to shoulder the unquantifiable cost of mass unhappiness. The Latvian economy is roughly 1% of the size of the UK's – yet our Baltic friends have four times as many hospital beds for young people with serious mental health problems per 100,000 than we do.[19] Considering the greater resources at our disposal, our failure seems more of an issue with priorities than cost.

Young people's mental health initiatives have to begin in preschool and continue until university and beyond. Harvard researchers suggest that 'toxic stress' – prolonged stress not ameliorated by a supportive adult – can have lasting mental health effects when it happens early in life.[20] As our brains develop over time, experiencing significant stress at an early age, such as abuse, poverty and poor care, can lead to chronic mental health conditions. These conditions can compound and become increasingly resistant to treatment. While early interventions are clearly preferable, most professionals that very young children interact with, including childcare providers and teachers, as well as many of their doctors, lack the expertise required to intervene.

Even those specifically trained to handle mental health issues in children are struggling to reach those who need help. A 2019 report found that despite referrals to England's children's mental health services surging, a quarter of all referrals are still being turned away.[21] This is over 130,000 young people not getting the treatment they need every year. Many of these refusals were because the patients' conditions were not deemed serious enough for treatment – despite many of them including young people who self-harm. They are turned away and rarely followed up on, meaning thousands of children fall through the net every year who could otherwise be on the path to a happy, healthy life.

Children's mental health should not be taken in isolation. Research suggests that a child's mental health is at least somewhat linked to that of their parents.[22] Adult mental health provision – including for addiction, depression and domestic abuse – rarely factors in the impact on the children of the families involved. A move towards whole-family treatment may be more effective than treating both adults and children in isolation.

For our schools, the government's plans are to fund a designated mental health lead for each school, train new support teams to help groups of schools, and attempt to slash waiting times for child mental health services. These moves will help, but they are too little, too late, and far too simple and unambitious. The charity YoungMinds points out that these measures will only help 'at most a quarter of the country in the next five years'.[23]

What schools *can* do

Sir Anthony Seldon, the former Vice-Chancellor of the University of Buckingham, Master of Wellington College and Head of Brighton College, is passionate about changing education from a negative to a positive influence on the mental health of children. 'All authority figures from the governors to the head down need to make it clear that every student is valued for who they are, not for the exam grades they achieve', he tells me. 'They should make it clear that bullying is totally unacceptable, and encourage an atmosphere of openness and honesty. The ten keys to happier living produced by Action for Happiness should be up in every classroom and corridor, and regularly discussed.'[24]

Sir Anthony argues that schools can do these things now – 'you don't need extra money'. It's not just the mental health of children that matters, it's the staff too. 'There's not a school in the world where the mental health of staff doesn't impinge on student wellbeing', Sir Anthony says.

Lucy Bailey, CEO of *Bounce Forward*, a charity that trains teachers to help students to develop the positive mental health traits that will help them to thrive in life, says that a cultural shift is required in our approach to mental health in schools. 'We continue to move deckchairs and skirt around the edges, using resources inefficiently', she says, adding that 'we know how to do it but we are working against a tide of tradition that benefits a few and pays lip service to many.'

Bounce Forward's 'Healthy Minds' project offers training and resources to teachers on resilience, relationships, social media usage and other topics related to mental health and wellbeing. The London

School of Economics analysed the effects of Healthy Minds through a trial involving 3500 secondary school pupils. Researchers found 'robust evidence' that when compared to standard Personal, Social, Health and Economic (PSHE) lessons, in which teachers receive little specialist training, the Healthy Minds approach improves participants' overall health, especially for boys, and 'increased the quality time its students spent with their family'.[25] Schools participating in the trial reported higher academic achievement and attendance and fewer exclusions among participating pupils.

Lucy argues that 'we talk about mental health but what we really mean is mental ill health. The two are connected but distinct.' Our approach to improving mental health should be far more focused on prevention, by encouraging healthy, resilient minds, rather than responding to problems once they arise. Prevention is not only more effective but a 'better use of resources.'

As a society we need to wake up to the fact that we have failed to provide our youngest generations with a meaningful, happy and mentally healthy life. We need to act fast – but without simply assuming that teachers or hashtags will take care of yet another societal problem, especially if we don't properly resource our schools. We simply cannot afford to not get mental health right. Everything else in this book depends on this.

Chapter 9:
Learning science

'Knowledge which is acquired
under compulsion obtains
no hold on the mind.'[1]
Plato

Benjamin Franklin, one of the most brilliant minds in history, once wrote in a letter that 'in this world nothing can be said to be certain, except death and taxes'. I'd like to add a third universal certainty – that everyone has a strong opinion on how education should be delivered.

This is understandable given that, at least today, nearly everyone in the West has the privilege of going to school. Many of us had good experiences, but some would rather forget their time within the school gates. Whichever camp you are in, you're bound to have strong views, regardless of how much time you've actually spent teaching.

So far I've discussed a few ways in which the education system is failing our teachers and students. While I hope you find my arguments convincing, I'm aware that I am just one voice among many. From Plato in the fourth century BC to Nick Gibb today (others may wish to make the obvious joke about our somewhat anachronistic Schools Minister here), there has never been a short supply of strong opinions on how education should be delivered. But there is one area that is only now entering mainstream discussions around education, and it's possibly the most important of all. Let's talk about the science of learning.

The brain is one of the most dynamic organisms on this planet. The image below is a connectome: a map of all the neuron connections in the brain, akin to a wiring diagram. It is rich and intricate and shows some of the vast complexity that ultimately gives rise to each individual.

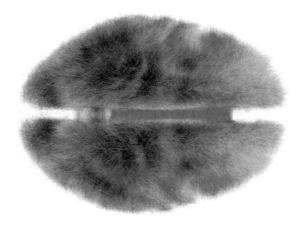

While each of us share the capacity to learn without restriction, the way in which we do this is varied. Understanding both the similarities and differences in the learning brain can profoundly benefit the learning process.

At its most basic, learning is about developing memory. To be clear, I do not only mean memory of specific facts, events, equations or laws, but also memory of processes and techniques, memory of problem-solving mechanisms, and memory of key tools and practices developed during the learning process.

Cognitive neuroscience is the scientific study of the biological processes that underpin cognitive functions. It combines cognitive science and neuroscience to help us understand thought, memory, learning and knowledge. Despite our brains being crucial to our very existence, 'cognitive neuroscience' as a distinct field has only been around for a few decades – the term was even reportedly coined in the back of a taxi[2]. The brain has always been a bit of a mystery, and in many ways it still is. But our understanding of how the mind works – and thus how we can best learn – has rapidly improved thanks to modern imaging techniques.

A brief historical journey will help us to understand just how recent our understanding of the brain is. The ancient Egyptians and some Greeks, such as Aristotle, thought the heart was responsible for thought. This belief stemmed from both religious myths and animal experiments, in which some animals could be seen to still move even after being decapitated. This view was disproven in the second century AD by Roman doctor Galen, but the misunderstanding, known as cardiocentric neurophysiology, persisted in some circles for millennia, requiring further refutation from modern-era thinkers such as René Descartes and William Harvey.[3] To this day we still instinctively refer to our hearts as being the source of our passions, emotions and soul, albeit metaphorically.

Later developments in neuroscience proved equally unscientific. Seventeenth-century English doctor Thomas Willis concluded that memory is stored in the area of the brain behind the forehead and temples, because that is where we rub when we are in deep thought.[4] The eighteenth century saw the rise of phrenology – the pseudoscientific view that mental traits can be inferred from the shape of the skull. In the nineteenth century, scientists began to localise functions in the brain through postmortem examinations of people suffering from physical and mental impairments. In the twentieth century, this view was increasingly challenged, as we began to learn how behaviours can be produced by many different areas of the brain.

As our understanding of the brain began to rapidly improve, scientists started to use this to delve deeper into how psychological functions like perception, knowledge and memory work. Cognitive neuroscience began to emerge as a distinct discipline from the 1950s, with progress turbocharged from the 1980s by the onset of far more advanced brain scanning techniques.[5] Today, scientists have a wealth of both experimental and theoretical methods for 'determining the nature of mind'.[6]

If our ability to understand the brain has radically transformed over the last few centuries, why do our schools still look roughly the same as they did when doctors were checking our heads for phrenological lumps?

We must understand the latest findings from cognitive neuroscience and learning science and embed them in our approach to education. After all, what are teachers if not overseers of developing minds? While understanding how the mind works is becoming increasingly important in teacher training, we are still not treating the subject with the seriousness it deserves. We wouldn't send newly qualified doctors into the job without a full understanding of how the healing process works, so why do we do this for teaching?

A comprehensive look at the neuroscientific foundations of learning is beyond the scope of this book. After all, while it's not rocket science, it's pretty close to brain surgery. However, there are a few important educational principles rooted in cutting-edge research that are worth exploring and which I have seen in practice during the development and adoption of CENTURY's learning tools.

The science of learning

Memory is the brain's faculty of storing and retrieving information. Memories can be short-lived or last many years, or be anything in between. *Short-term, working memory* is information that we hold for a short time only. A good example of this is a set of instructions we hold in our working memory in order to act on them. Once the task is done, the set of instructions is forgotten. *Long-term memory* is the function of storing information to recall it after the event. There are three parts to this function: the encoding of the information, when it is first acquired; the storage of it; and the retrieval or remembering of the information at a later time.

Teachers and indeed parents should care about memory because long-term memory is what we are primarily interested in when we are talking about teaching and learning. Let me use an example to illustrate my point. When a teacher first introduces Pythagoras' theorem to their pupils in a Maths class, a brand new set of connections is created in the brain of each pupil. As the pupils listen to the teacher's explanations and start to solve problems, they *encode* the information and the new connections coalesce into a unique pathway of neurons. It is this pathway which itself *stores* the memory for later use. Next time a pupil comes to a problem that makes use of Pythagoras' theorem, they need to *retrieve* the memory of what they learned in the lesson. The pupil does this by activating the pathway that was originally encoded.

The learning process can impede or enhance the formation of long-term memories, and therefore can impede or enhance learning itself. Most teachers will be familiar with the pride of teaching a pupil something new and watching them seemingly master it during the course of the lesson, only for this pride to turn to abject frustration when by the next lesson everything has been forgotten. This is a very natural part of memory formation: when a pathway is first formed, it is a fragile thing that is easily lost.

When we recall the same piece of information multiple times, the synapses between neurons (the neuronal junction) strengthen and the ease of recalling information increases. The strengthening of synapses is a physical process that happens in the brain and it is this mechanism that is thought to underpin learning and memory.

Cognitive load theory

Previously, we discussed the idea of cognitive load. This refers to the cognitive effort (or amount of information processing) required by a person to perform a task. The theory is that when one's short-term or working memory capacity is exceeded during learning, it will lead to working memory failure and will hamper learning.

Cognitive load theory is based on the idea that the brain is limited in the amount of information that it can process at one time. Evidence behind the theory shows that it is possible to overload the brain by taking up all the available working memory space, resulting in an inability to process new information or to encode it to long-term memory.

A 1973 study that found one of the most important reasons why grandmaster chess players are better than novice players is because of their superior memory.[7] Players were shown a chess board with pieces arranged in a plausible way and then asked to recall the position of the pieces. Then the task was repeated, but with the chess pieces arranged randomly. The grandmaster players significantly outperformed the novices when recalling the order for the plausible scenarios, but not for the random ones. Researchers concluded that this was because the grandmaster players had memorised all plausible chess board scenarios. They were able to recall from their vaster long-term memory stores, while the novice players were reliant on their shallower working memory. Where the experts used knowledge, the novices used working memory. The latter is soon depleted when doing tasks, while the experts' working memory is freed up to allow them to complete more complex operations.

Tom Needham, an English teacher who has written about how an understanding of cognitive load can improve teaching, suggests the implications of this study for schools are 'striking'.[8] Teachers should spend most of their time expanding pupils' knowledge so that they are able to 'overcome the seemingly unalterable capacity in their short-term memory and instead recall, apply and use relevant knowledge from their long-term memories'. This doesn't mean adding tomes of content to an already bloated curriculum – it means using what we are learning about how the brain works to get the most out of our students.

Cognitive load theory also suggests that teaching and learning should be designed in a way that doesn't unnecessarily overload a pupil's working memory. Mark Enser, a teacher, describes how 'overly complex instructions, distractions in our environment or being given too much additional information' can raise extraneous load – reducing pupils' ability to learn.[9] Teachers need to be careful not to cognitively overload the pupil with unnecessary information or poorly designed materials, but they also need to make sure that the material is sufficiently difficult to optimise memory formation.

Cognitive load theory is becoming a mainstream part of education, so much so that Ofsted is using it as part of its inspection framework.[10] Some have suggested that if Ofsted likes it, then something must be wrong. But I disagree. Teachers themselves are leading the cognitive load charge, to the benefit of students.

Interleaving

German psychologist Hermann Ebbinghaus was a pioneer of measuring memory and conducted hundreds of experiments on himself to discover the rate at which we forget information. In these experiments he taught himself lists of meaningless nonsense syllables, such as 'wid' and 'zof', and tested himself on them at varying intervals in order to understand more about memory and forgetting. After learning a list of syllables once, the rate of forgetting is steep. But if the material is reviewed over certain time intervals, the curve gets shallower. Each review means that information is retained for longer and longer.

Ebbinghaus' research is a good demonstration of why 'cramming', or studying material in one big chunk, isn't an effective method of learning. The idea that material is learned well when cramming is an illusion: as well as being mind-numbingly boring, it's a rubbish way to learn.

Interleaved learning involves spreading out topics by intermixing them with other topics. For example, rather than studying English, maths and science for an hour each, interleaving suggests it is preferable to break this down into 20 minute sessions for each subject, before repeating. This method can better commit information to the long-term memory by allowing the appropriate level of forgetting to occur before the information is retrieved, which increases the likelihood of it being stored in the long-term memory. Interleaved learning also improves the ability to transfer knowledge across subjects by better establishing specific links between areas, further improving learning.

The effects of anything as delicate as how students learn is hard to quantify, but studies do show that interleaving boosts outcomes. Psychology professor Doug Rohrer has found that 'interleaving produced better scores on final tests of learning'.[11] He suggests the practice encourages pupils to consider different solutions to different problems, whereas studying the same topic repeatedly can cause learners to assume what worked for the previous problem will work for the next.

An understanding of memory is important not just for teachers, but for technology and resource design too. The historic inability of technology to transform education can partly be blamed on a poor understanding of the learning process. When I founded CENTURY, I wanted to be sure that anything we offer to schools is based on a deep understanding of how children learn. My team has used these theories about memory, alongside AI, to develop technology that learns an individual's working memory, long-term memory and the optimal time to space the learning, so that retrieval becomes more efficient. CENTURY promotes long-term information retention by including short tests at the end of each 'nugget' of learning, encouraging learners to revisit previously completed work, and interspersing nuggets from different subjects on students' individual learning paths.

Sleep

In his excellent book *Why We Sleep*, neuroscience professor Matthew Walker argues that a lack of sleep is the 'greatest public health challenge' facing developed nations this century.[12] A certain pandemic might have shunted sleep down the pecking order – but lack of sleep is still hugely damaging, especially to children's learning and development.

Our children are sleepwalking into crisis, almost literally. One in four children are sleep deprived, with a whopping 42% of 15 year olds – at one of the most crucial times of their education – being 'too tired to concentrate on their lessons'.[13] Prescriptions for melatonin sleeping tablets for children soared tenfold from 2007 to 2017, while hospital admissions for children with sleep disorders tripled.[14] Everything from smartphones to our diets to later bedtimes have been blamed – but whatever the cause, the impact on children's education (let alone their health) is real.

Scientifically, sleep is somewhat of a mystery, but it is believed that it plays a crucial role in the formation of our memories. Scientists aren't entirely sure how, but they suggest that memories are consolidated while we snooze, as sleeping strengthens the connections in our brain that result in memory. Different types of memories are consolidated during different stages of sleep. One theory is that complex memories are acquired during rapid-eye-movement (REM) sleep – usually when we dream – while new information is believed to be stored during slow-wave sleep (SWS), when we are in a deep sleep.

Sleep deprivation reduces our ability to both encode information and store it as a memory. When we are chronically tired, we are less able to focus, and our ability to recall existing memories is hampered. This is a difficult area for empirical measurement, but some studies using rats have suggested that being deprived of REM sleep results in poorer performance in learning tasks.[15]

The implications for our future education systems are enormous. What is the point of a perfectly designed curriculum, motivated and freed teachers, and a low-stress exam system if students turn up to school too exhausted to learn?

One proposed solution is to start the school day an hour later so that children can get extra sleep. The French government has taken the bold step of giving its teenagers an extra hour in bed, after research showed that more sleep can lead to better exam results.[16] But I'm not convinced that this is the answer. As we have discussed, the causes of the sleep crisis are largely behavioural – we're using our smartphones too much too late in the day, among other causes. If you tell a teenager they can get up an hour later in the morning, the vast majority of them will simply stay up an hour later the night before.

This is one area for which teachers are definitely not responsible, but it doesn't seem too far-fetched to imagine a future Education Secretary demanding all teachers tuck their pupils into bed and read them a goodnight story each night. The solution to this problem is simply better parenting. Parents need to take greater responsibility by regulating their children's access to social media and mobile devices in the home, and by ensuring that they get a good night's sleep. Half of all children sleep with a mobile phone by their bed, with the same proportion saying that they would be lost without access to their phone.[17] We cannot expect children to stop doing this by their own accord, especially as many apps are designed to be addictive, and nor can teachers pry phones from the hands of tucked-up teens. Until we parents get real about the problems we are storing up for our children and their teachers, educational success will always be out of reach.

Metacognition and mindset

Teaching is not the only ingredient in academic success – how you think about learning might matter, too.

Metacognition is the broad term used to describe the awareness and understanding of one's own thought processes. Examples of educationally-relevant metacognitive skills include evaluating your progress on a task, identifying appropriate strategies to solve a problem, assessing your own ability and self-correcting based on this. For example, it is metacognitive skills that help you decide whether it's better to revise for your Maths mock exam or complete your History reading when you only have time for one. Experimental evidence suggests that improvements in learning can be achieved by encouraging proficiency in these sorts of skills.

It's not hard to see why this might be the case; what a pupil thinks about learning, their own abilities and the accuracy of their assessments of themselves will have a profound effect on their behaviour. The pupil who correctly identifies that they are halfway through a task, or who is accurate about how well they have understood a topic, is the one who is going to put their time to better use than the pupil who is incorrect in their thinking about these things.

An influential 2007 study found that students who believed that their intelligence levels are set in stone performed worse than those who believed that intelligence can grow.[18] The study also found that the latter position, which has become known as a 'growth mindset', can also improve classroom motivation.

Growth mindset is the idea that intelligence can be changed or 'grown' by working effectively: effort will lead to success. A *fixed mindset* of intelligence is the belief that intelligence is innate, similar to height; you have what you are born with and that's it. This difference has big implications for the classroom and that is part of the reason why this theory has gained so much traction in the last decade. A child with a fixed mindset of intelligence sees no value in making an effort. If they cannot achieve success on the first try, then they are incapable of achieving success. Full stop. These children feel they have no control over whether or not they *are* clever, so all they can control is whether they *seem* clever. While disruptive behaviour in the classroom has many causes, it's easy to see how having a fixed mindset can be one of them: the child sees no value in making an effort and may give up at the first setback.

Typical growth mindset interventions are for the teacher or parent to 'praise the process, not the person', commending the way a problem has been solved rather than on the child being clever. They also emphasise the importance of a child working hard, adapting their strategies, learning from previous mistakes and not giving up. These are the things we must praise when we see them at home and in the classroom, and these are the things we must encourage when we don't see them.

But all is not rosy with the growth mindset. A study published in *Psychological Science* this year found 'little to no evidence for the major premises of mindset theory', with its major findings directly contradicting the theory.[19] In response to these and similar findings, growth mindset pioneer Carol Dweck said that the theory appears to be 'even more complex than we imagined'.[20] She remains insistent that, when applied correctly, and in the right circumstances, a growth mindset can have a transformative effect for student outcomes. Data analysis by CENTURY on attitudes to learning and outcomes supports this view.

Some might be tempted to dismiss concepts like growth mindset and other metacognitive skills as 'soft' skills, as if something as crucial as how a child views their ability to develop is unimportant. But as Glenn Whitman and Ian Kelleher argue in their brilliant book *Neuroteach: Brain Science and the Future of Education*, terms like 'soft' do 'not do justice to how greatly these skills can affect student performance'.[21] The authors argue that the evidence shows clear links between 'a student's mindset and his or her academic performance', as well as their ability to face 'the most difficult learning challenges'. While not yet settled, the mindset debate could have big implications for the success of our learners.

Lifelong learning

Leaving aside the science of learning, let me propose a more fundamental rethinking of how we approach learning. When we think of education, we often think of a teacher delivering a lesson to a young student. Education and school don't usually conjure up images of students thinking for themselves about what they want to learn or explore next, forging their own educational pathway. But in order for our educational operating system to be fit for purpose, we have to ensure that every child becomes a willing participant in lifelong learning.

If you were to ask anyone on the street when they think that education ends, most would say either after school or university. For decades, if not centuries, this was an acceptable view, although far from ideal. But as we have discussed, the coming decades are going to see a radical transformation in both the skills required to work and the number of different roles humans will be expected to play. Phillip Brown, Professor of Sociology at Cardiff University, has outlined how technological change means we face 'a need for educational reform and a greater focus on lifelong learning'.[22] Brown argues that the 'frontloading' of education during childhood and early adolescence is based on 'the assumption that relatively limited reskilling or upskilling will be required later in working life'. Unless we change course radically, our education system itself will hamstring our efforts to survive in a rapidly changing jobs market.

The data on adult education suggests we are losing the battle to upskill as adults. In 2020, the *Learning and Work Institute* found that the number of British adults taking part in some form of learning is at its lowest on record, and has plunged by 4 million in the last decade.[23] Just one in three adults took part in learning in the last three years. This isn't just formal learning that leads to tangible qualifications, either – 'learning' here is defined as 'practising, studying or reading about something', whether at home, at work or at a college, formal or informal. Of those who haven't 'learned' since leaving full-time education, only 17% said they would be likely to learn ever again in the future. Almost half of those unemployed have not taken part in any learning since finishing their full-time education.

Our focus must be on those most in need of help. The wealthy among us, as always, will have more access to, and less need of, support. We need to ensure we promote lifelong learning across the board or we will end up seeing social mobility plummet.

Crucial to this will be to promote ambition. If, like me, you've had to sit through more than your fair share of corporate motivational talks, you'll have been bored to death by talk of passion, drive and motivation. These are serious topics, however – Gallup found that 85% of employees are 'not engaged or actively disengaged at work'.[24] This doesn't just waste a serious amount of time and human potential, Gallup suggests it costs us $7 trillion in lost productivity.

If we as adults are trying to promote motivation and engagement as fundamental to success, why are teachers not more supported to build it into the delivery of education? Can school be a place where we encourage all children to strive? Can we even teach ambition? Motivation is complex and children in particular are motivated in complex ways. We don't yet have a complete picture of motivation, but competition, curiosity, intrinsic and extrinsic reward, and social contagion can all combine to motivate us in different ways.[25]

I once visited a school in London to share my entrepreneurial story with a group of children. This was when I was first researching how to use technology to improve education, so my eyes were peeled for any potential problems to solve. During the session I asked the kids what they wanted to be when they grew up. I remember so many confident voices saying 'doctor', 'lawyer', 'professional footballer' and 'racing car driver'. In contrast, when I asked the same question in a school in a more deprived part of London and only a few kids even wanted to put their hands up. The professions they mentioned were more vague, like 'I want to be in business'. One said he aimed to get a job at a supermarket like his Dad.

This is a really complex problem, partly to do with role models and how ambition is talked about at home, as well as the fixed versus growth mindset we discussed earlier. But there is no point in society pointing to the home and saying it's solely an issue for parents, because that's unlikely to help things change, at least as rapidly as they need to. Even in some households in which you might think children are taught to be ambitious, how many times do children say 'Mummy, I'm bad at maths' only to hear 'Don't worry darling, you get that from me'? This completely undoes the growth mindset efforts of the teacher.

The problem of motivation is also related to cognitive science. Psychologist Daniel T. Willingham points out that the reason children often don't like school is because school is designed in a way that the brain doesn't find rewarding, so children switch off.[26]

We have to enrich a child's experience at school, which allows them to see what is available to them in society. This is easier said than done with the bloated curriculum, burned-out teachers and poorly designed education system we have discussed, as well as funding pressures. But if we could embed ambition in education, what would it look like? In an ideal world, this sort of motivational training would take place in the classroom frequently. As often already happens in the best schools, local business people, community leaders, parents and alumni could take a far greater role in inspiring and motivating students. A freed-up teacher would have the time to set their children free to work on projects that are relevant to their lives and passions.

Fields such as educational cognitive neuroscience are still young, but their findings are already having massive implications for how we teach children and how they learn. Lessons from cognitive neuroscience are being embedded in teacher training across the world, while further trials of concepts like the growth mindset will help us to move towards the successful education system that our teachers and children deserve.

Chapter 10: Education 4.0

'I never worry about action,
but only about inaction.'[1]
Winston Churchill

There are some things about education that everyone takes for granted, but no one quite knows why they still exist. Many aspects of schooling once made good sense in times gone by, but are perhaps due for a rethink today. So much of what we do has been driven by the resources available at one time or another as government budgets have fluctuated. Others are curious accidents of history. But some make no sense at all.

Most of the troublesome aspects of education that we have discussed had well-intentioned beginnings. Yet for any progress to be made, someone still has to ask why we do things, as unpopular a question as that may be.

You might have gathered that, given both the scale and importance of the problems we face, I don't believe that the solution lies in simply enacting a few new education laws, chucking a bit more cash at schools and being a bit nicer to our teachers. These are all vital. But we require a revolution in our educational operating system – not some bolt-on upgrades and not simply turning it off and on again and hoping it fixes itself.

Writing about the world of business, PayPal founder Peter Thiel describes how copying existing innovations 'takes the world from 1 to *n*, adding more of something familiar', while creating something new takes us from 0 to 1 – the creation of something radically new.[2] Thiel says that 'today's "best practices" lead to dead ends; the best paths are new and untried'. This is the challenge facing those of us interested in creating an education system that is fit for purpose. Radical change is needed, not minor improvements. Thiel argues that forging a successful new path in any sector takes nothing short of a miracle, yet miracles are a currency unique to humans – we just tend to refer to them as 'technology' or 'innovation'.

We tend to associate innovation and reform as being led either by individual visionaries, mass movements or government initiatives. It's true that these forces can play important roles in innovation. Every age has had its Elon Musk to be grateful for, labour movements have radically improved working conditions for billions of people, and governments have played a crucial role in the development of technologies from the internet to space travel. The latter point is made forcefully by the economist Mariana Mazzucato, who argues that the state has always played a crucial role in innovation, taking 'the risks that businesses won't'.[3]

While this is true, many of the biggest transformations in history have arisen from everyday people like me and you who are simply fed up with the status quo. Railways, computers, cars, mobile phones and even the printing press owe far more to the hard work and brilliance of people who thought our existing lot could be improved than they do to any formal research programme. Innovation is far more 'bottom up' than 'top down' – and that which drives lasting change is always predicated on a real need.

Anton Howes, a historian of innovation at the Royal Society of Arts, suggests that innovation is contagious. He says the acceleration in British innovation after the sixteenth century was caused at least partly by the 'emergence and spread of an improving mentality' – a mindset that 'saw room for improvement where others saw none'.[4] Inventors, reformers and innovators became 'evangelists' for improvement, giving birth to centuries of unprecedented social change and economic growth. We must take inspiration from our proud history of innovators and reformers and become evangelists for an education system that is fit for purpose.

Creating the future

What education will look like in the decades to come is, at present, unknown – one of Rumsfeld's 'known unknowns'. But, as the overused yet valuable saying goes, the best way to predict the future is to create it. 'Creating it' here does not imply enacting a series of government bills to reshape the education system. Our ambitions are greater and more sophisticated than that of a bureaucrat's pen. Creating a system that is fit for purpose in a world transformed by technology and innovation will require the collective, focused efforts of parents, teachers, educationalists and policy-makers.

This system should include:

1. A vastly slimmed-down curriculum that liberates teachers to focus on the knowledge and skills required to thrive in a rapidly changing, uncertain world.
2. Replacing an inefficacious and stressful exam system with lower-stakes tests enabled by technology, which provide a far greater and detailed picture of the individual.
3. Trusting teachers with freedom to do what they actually joined the profession to do – teach and nurture our young minds.
4. Students and teachers that are mentally healthy, motivated and supported.
5. Learning that is based on the latest advances in neuroscience and augmented by advanced technologies like AI.

These are all eminently achievable, well within our grasp and in many cases at least cost-neutral. Achieving them is just a question of our will.

We need to inject a sense of urgency into our efforts to reform education. Equally, we must put aside ideological differences and focus on working for the betterment of children. Regardless of one's viewpoint, few can argue that the current system is fit for purpose. We must pool our collective passions and imaginations, distilled through the filter of research and evidence, and make lasting changes. The coronavirus pandemic is the defining moment of this generation, the biggest upheaval the world at large has seen for decades. For the benefit of our children, there is no better time than now to make a change. We shouldn't shy away from the opportunity before us – being forced out of our comfort zone by a devastating virus should serve as a catalyst for changing parts of our society that have held us back for generations.

Follow the data

While the ideas for reform I have proposed are, where possible, backed up by evidence, they are just that – ideas. To find out what works, you need a culture of experiment and trial. One of the most promising developments in recent British educational history was the creation of the Education Endowment Foundation (EEF), an independent charity that aims to foster and fund randomised controlled trials across the system. The EEF tests a diverse variety of pedagogical programmes, from *Philosophy for Children* to phonics programmes such as *Read Write Inc* to chess classes. However, it is handicapped by a critical limitation: it cannot easily test broad structural changes that affect an entire set of schools, though it is currently working with UCL on a pilot study looking at optimal practices related to setting and mixed-ability teaching.

The problem is both structural and ethical. Let me illustrate. Let's say I want to run an experiment concerning teacher workload, the crisis we discussed earlier. The aim might be to study the effects of removing common mandatory requirements for teachers on student achievement, teacher retention and teacher recruitment. To do this, we recruit a set of schools, half of which abolish all marking, planning, assessment, display and classroom-layout policies, while the other half serves as a control by maintaining existing practice. Teachers would monitor their weekly working hours via diaries and would have to keep within a limit of 40 hours per week.

This is evidently a risky experiment for headteachers to participate in: what if they get assigned to the experimental group and it all goes wrong? They could easily be looked askance at by Ofsted and others for having relinquished valued forms of control so easily. Furthermore, the experiment would probably need to run for at least a couple years for the effects of the intervention to really embed themselves in schools, and for any effect on retention and recruitment to be noticeable. So an obvious incentive to get schools to participate would be the guarantee of a holiday from Ofsted inspections during the experimental period, while ensuring that this isn't abused by poorly performing schools. This might also be necessary to ensure the experiment's validity; otherwise particularly paranoid schools might participate but still unofficially make teachers do all the same things they used to do. There are also a number of ethical questions that arise from using students as guinea pigs.

Already this is starting to look like the sort of experiment that would be very tricky to organise within existing structures. The actual organisation and evaluation could be done by the EEF, but you'd need buy-in from Ofsted, parents, and of course the leadership of various multi-academy trusts. Some MATs would no doubt be not entirely thrilled at the thought of some schools within their organisation diverging so massively from their general way of doing business. So this kind of large-scale structural experiment never really gets done and the EEF sticks to doing high-quality evaluations of very specific pedagogical programmes.

The problem with this is that it doesn't give you a useful blueprint for fixing endemic problems across the whole system, it just produces a grab-bag of tested interventions for heads to select. The EEF is really good at telling you what the optimal layout is for the deckchairs on the Titanic, but we don't have a way of doing the kinds of policy experiments that would allow us to stop the ship from sinking.

Experimentation lies at the core of innovation. It's a huge part of an entrepreneurial mindset, but one that runs contrary to the world of education, which generally sticks to the tried and tested. This approach would be rational if our educational customs were actually robustly evidence-based, but they almost never are and owe far more to historical flukes than sensible design or slow evolutionary processes. There was a time in the recent past when it looked as though we might finally enter a world where we let a thousand flowers bloom and see what flourished, but sadly we decided that real experimentation was the one thing we could not bear. Experiments involving children's education may be unpalatable to the squeamish. I appreciate the need for the most robust ethical protections; any experiments involving children and education must be bound by strict ethical guidelines. But what makes me really squirm is the thought of millions of children being let down, generation after generation, because we were too timid to try something new.

Fear of the unknown is understandable, but in the world of education it doesn't really make any sense. In a world where so little of what we do now is robustly evidence-based, there's no actual reason to have a strong preference for the status quo. To use a medical analogy, very sick people are generally much happier to try out experimental medicines than very healthy people, because they have much less to lose. I would argue that the state of play in education is such that our schools are much more similar to the very sick patients than the very healthy volunteers.

We must begin a new era of courage and bravery. We must get beyond the 'let's do what we've always done' mantra, and put some time and money into finding out what actually works. We will need to take a few risks – but nothing of value has ever been produced without risk.

Education 4.0

Human life has arguably changed more in the last few centuries than it has in our entire existence. The biggest modern changes have been the result of three distinct industrial revolutions (some break these down into further sub-revolutions). The first saw the dawn of steam and water-powered machines revolutionising production. The second saw railway and the telegraph transforming the transmission of both people and information, as well as electricity overhauling production. The third was the digital revolution – the rise of computers and intelligent machines impacting every aspect of our lives.

That brings us to the present day. We are entering a fourth industrial revolution, in which advanced technologies like artificial intelligence are changing the nature of existence beyond what we can even imagine. This will include practical innovations such as smart factories, in which advanced robotics and big data will be used to radically improve efficiency and lower costs. It will also include hyper-futuristic areas like advanced synthetic biology – the creation of new organisms by writing DNA. Klaus Schwab, founder of the World Economic Forum and coiner of the term 'fourth industrial revolution', argues that the effects of Industry 4.0 may eclipse its predecessors. He points out that while the cloth spindle took over a century to reach factories outside of Europe, the internet 'permeated across the globe in less than a decade'.[5]

In terms of its scale and ambition, we require nothing short of an Education 4.0. By this I don't mean simply the application of fourth industrial technology to education – far from it. Technology will continue to transform education, but it will never replace the beating heart of learning that is fundamentally human. Education is not industry and must be treated differently.

The speed of technological advancement is increasing rapidly, in turn accelerating the speed of our everyday lives. The writer and policy thinker Robert Colvile calls this 'the great acceleration'.[6] From our work schedules to our thoughts to how we communicate, we are stretching the limits of our minds by putting the mental pedal far too close to the metal. While this results in innovations that improve our wellbeing, it also has serious implications for our social stability and life satisfaction. Colvile argues that the great acceleration is harming social interaction, making us all more impatient, frustrated and atomised.

Education 4.0, therefore, must allow the process of learning to take place at a speed at which humans flourish. Where Education 4.0 differs from Industry 4.0 is that it must harness the power of technology at a human scale, at a naturally human speed. Children are not factory workers, nodes of public transport or handheld devices. Their fragile, developing minds must be treated with care and love – qualities that only a human operating at human speeds can offer. Education 4.0 must embrace the power of a good teacher, but provide them with the freedom, resources and technology they need to do their job effectively. It must recognise that the new world appearing on the horizon requires a radical rethink of what education is for. It must embrace principles of learning science and encourage lifelong learning. But Education 4.0 is as much about what we don't need as what we do need, and we certainly don't need the bloated curricula, suffocating accountability system and tinkering politicians that we have discussed.

Here, some readers may have expected me, as an educational AI entrepreneur, to wax lyrical about how AI holds the key to a brighter future. To be clear, I am in full agreement with Sir Anthony Seldon when he suggests that AI will 'carry humans' even further than revolutionary technologies such as the car.[7] This is true of AI's potential for education as it is for all other sectors. But the education system we require should harness the power of AI, rather than depend on it. AI can liberate teachers and personalise education. It cannot assess the nuances in long-form writing, let alone comfort an upset child or inspire one to achieve greatness by itself.

Schools should be founded on human-to-human interaction complemented and augmented by advanced learning technologies. When students arrive at school every morning, we should be able to use big data to tell them exactly which room to visit to address their individual learning needs. Our current system is more rigid than a Swiss railway timetable – it is ludicrous that we know where our kids will be sitting and what they might be learning at 11:30am on the 6th of April next year. But for all the potential of technology, in those rooms it is vital that learning technologies should be side-by-side with excellent human teachers, whose care and support are axiomatic aspects of learning.

A choice

Recalling my opening salvo against the educational orthodoxy, it is vital that teachers and parents are the foundation of any attempt to reform education. Who else could know a child's needs better than their parents and their teachers? Certainly not a Prime Minister, an Education Secretary or a bureaucrat – or even me, for that matter.

But, as a society, we face a choice. We can continue to send our children to schools that aren't preparing them for life in a rapidly changing world. We can continue to shackle our teachers to a crumbling education system, suffocating their passions and smothering their good intentions. We can continue to convince ourselves that we are doing the best we possibly can for our children, despite the mounting evidence to the contrary.

Or, remembering that the guarantee of inertia is worse than the potential of failure, we can choose to become evangelists for innovation. We can choose to be as bold in dismantling a failed system as we can be in building a better one. We can choose to be brave in trying new approaches, taking calculated risks in the hope of a brighter future.

What will you choose to do?

Endnotes

Foreword

1. https://www.thetimes.co.uk/article/coronavirus-700-000-children-doing-no-school-work-qprsc9z23

2. https://www.theguardian.com/education/2020/jun/03/decade-of-progress-tackling-uk-pupil-disadvantage-wiped-out-coronavirus-school-closures

3. https://www.bbc.co.uk/news/education-53514564

4. https://www.pwc.co.uk/services/economics/insights/the-impact-of-automation-on-jobs.html

5. https://www.ft.com/content/96e43c16-f592-11e9-bbe1-4db3476c5ff0

6. https://literacytrust.org.uk/parents-and-families/adult-literacy/

7. https://www.nationalnumeracy.org.uk/sites/default/files/nn124_essentials_numeracyreport_for_web.pdf

8. https://assets.publishing.service.gov.uk/government/uploads/system/uploads/attachment_data/file/746493/ESS_2017_UK_Report_Controlled_v06.00.pdf

9. https://www.ft.com/content/3cea8516-8963-11e5-90de-f44762bf9896

10. https://www.pwc.co.uk/economic-services/assets/international-impact-of-automation-feb-2018.pdf

11. https://www.edge.co.uk/sites/default/files/documents/skills_shortage_bulletin_5_final_-_web.pdf

12. https://www.gov.uk/government/news/adults-skills-gap

Introduction

1. https://www.gov.uk/government/publications/state-funded-schools-inspections-and-outcomes-as-at-31-march-2020/main-findings-state-funded-schools-inspections-and-outcomes-as-at-31-march-2020

2. Roser, M. and Ortiz-Ospina, E. (2020) 'Literacy', published online at OurWorldInData.org.

3. Akçomak S., Webbink D. and Weel, B. (2016) 'Why Did the Netherlands Develop So Early? The Legacy of the Brethren of the Common Life', *The Economic Journal*, 126 (593), 821–860, https://doi.org/10.1111/ecoj.12193.

4. https://apnews.com/Business%20Wire/d7d10eb8c3cb4ee1bb757abf3a2c5421

Chapter 1 The new operating system

1   https://gs.statcounter.com/windows-version-market-share/desktop/worldwide/#monthly-201802-202001

2   https://www.publictechnology.net/articles/news/nhs-still-running-2300-pcs-windows-xp

3   https://news.microsoft.com/2001/10/25/windows-xp-is-here/

4   Readers from nations beyond the UK may be interested to know that the dispute over the so-called 'pasty tax' is a real thing that happened, and was a surprisingly large feature in debates over the Budget of 2012.

5   See for example Spector, P. E. (1986) 'Perceived Control by Employees: A Meta-Analysis of Studies Concerning Autonomy and Participation at Work', *Human Relations*, 39 (11), 1005–1016, https://doi.org/10.1177/001872678603901104.

6   https://www.telegraph.co.uk/news/2016/08/28/three-rs-on-the-decline-as-a-quarter-of-adults-have-a-reading-ag/

7   https://www.ifs.org.uk/uploads/publications/comms/R126.pdf

8   Torrance, H. (2018) 'The Return to Final Paper Examining in English National Curriculum Assessment and School Examinations: Issues of Validity, Accountability and Politics', *British Journal of Educational Studies*, 66 (1), 3–27, https://doi.org/10.1080/00071005.2017.1322683.

9   Jones, I., Wheadon, C., Humphries, S. and Inglis, M. (2016) 'Fifty Years of A-level Mathematics: Have Standards Changed?', *British Education Research Journal*, 42, 543–560, https://doi.org/10.1002/berj.3224.

10   https://www.buckingham.ac.uk/wp-content/uploads/2010/11/A-Levels-2012.pdf

11   https://nces.ed.gov/fastfacts/display.asp?id=38

12   https://www.npr.org/sections/ed/2016/04/21/474850688/9-out-of-10-parents-think-their-kids-are-on-grade-level-theyre-probably-wrong?t=1588606928590

13   For example, see Hulme, C. and Snowling, M. J. (2013) 'Learning to Read: What we Know and What we Need to Understand Better', *Child Development Perspectives* , 7 (1), 1–5.

14   https://www.telegraph.co.uk/education/0/a-level-grades-should-be-abolished-to-remedy-our-failing-exam-sy/

15   https://www.parentkind.org.uk/Research--Policy/Research/Annual-Parent-Survey-2018

Chapter 2 Why do we send our children to school?

1   https://en.unesco.org/covid19/educationresponse

2   https://www.varkeyfoundation.org/media/4790/gts-index-9-11-2018.pdf

3   https://schoolsweek.co.uk/indecent-proposals-111-curriculum-suggestions-made-to-schools-this-year/

4   https://www.independent.co.uk/sport/militants-mob-blunkett-in-schools-strike-protest-1615825.html

5   https://www.nytimes.com/2020/01/21/books/review/slaying-goliath-diane-ravitch.html

6   http://www.utcmediacityuk.org.uk/parents-fear-children-wont-find-jobs/

7   https://www.varkeyfoundation.org/media/4340/vf-parents-survey-18-single-pages-for-flipbook.pdf

8   https://www.barnardos.org.uk/news/survey-reveals-childrens-top-back-school-anxieties

9   http://www.asianews.it/news-en/For-some-youths,-suicide-is-better-than-going-back-to-school-44717.html

10   https://www.bbc.co.uk/news/world-asia-50693777

11   https://archive.defense.gov/Transcripts/Transcript.aspx?TranscriptID=2636

Chapter 3 Graduating in 2030

1   Grove, A. S. (1996) *Only the Paranoid Survive: How to Exploit the Crisis Points that Challenge Every Company and Career.* New York: Currency Doubleday.

2   https://www.inc.com/jessica-stillman/12-hilariously-wrong-tech-predictions.html

3   James, L. (1995) *Nobel Laureates In Chemistry,* 1901–1992. Washington, DC: American Chemical Society.

4   https://www.mckinsey.com/featured-insights/future-of-work/jobs-lost-jobs-gained-what-the-future-of-work-will-mean-for-jobs-skills-and-wages

5   https://data.worldbank.org/indicator/SL.TLF.TOTL.IN

6   https://markets.businessinsider.com/news/stocks/joe-biden-to-coal-miners-learn-to-code-1028794296

7   https://reason.com/2019/03/11/learn-to-code-twitter-harassment-ross/

8   https://www.mckinsey.com/featured-insights/future-of-work/jobs-lost-jobs-gained-what-the-future-of-work-will-mean-for-jobs-skills-and-wages

9   http://www3.weforum.org/docs/WEF_Future_of_Jobs_2018.pdf

10   Susskind, R. and Susskind, D. (2017) *The Future of the Professions: How Technology will Transform the Work of Human Experts.* New York, NY: Oxford University Press.

11   https://www.bbc.co.uk/news/business-52364811

12   https://impact.chartered.college/article/skills-versus-knowledge-curriculum-debate-matters-one-need-reject/

13   Reif, F. (2010) *Applying Cognitive Science to Education.* Cambridge, MA: MIT Press.

14   Willingham, D. (2010) *Why Don't Students Like School?* San Francisco, CA: Jossey Bass.

15   https://daisychristodoulou.com/2013/10/false-dichotomies-begging-the-question-and-the-knowledge-skills-debate/

16   https://www.appg-ai.org/evidence/theme-reports/learning-to-learn-the-future-proof-skill/

17   Senge, P. (2006) *The Fifth Discipline*. London: Random House.

18   https://www.mckinsey.com/featured-insights/future-of-work/ai-automation-and-the-future-of-work-ten-things-to-solve-for

19   Harari, Y., 2016. Homo Deus: A Brief History Of Tomorrow. Harvill Secker, p.326.

20   https://www.wsj.com/articles/the-hybrid-skills-that-tomorrows-jobs-will-require-11547994266

21   https://www.independent.co.uk/news/uk/home-news/universal-basic-income-ubi-scotland-uk-nicola-sturgeon-coronavirus-a9498076.html

22   https://www.mckinsey.com/featured-insights/future-of-work/ai-automation-and-the-future-of-work-ten-things-to-solve-for

23   Deming, D. J. (2017) 'The Growing Importance of Social Skills in the Labor Market', *The Quarterly Journal of Economics*, 132 (4), 1593–1640.

24   https://media.nesta.org.uk/documents/the_future_of_skills_employment_in_2030_0.pdf

25   https://www.edsk.org/publications/free-to-choose/

26   https://impact.chartered.college/article/the-learning-skills-curriculum-raising-the-bar-closing-the-gap-at-gcse/

Chapter 4 Artificial intelligence

1   https://yougov.co.uk/topics/philosophy/trackers/how-intelligent-brits-think-robots-are

2   https://assets.publishing.service.gov.uk/government/uploads/system/uploads/attachment_data/file/802548/BEIS_AI_PR_Survey_40309009_Topline_summary_V1__1_.pdf

3   https://www.businessinsider.com/founders-fund-the-future-2011-7?r=US&IR=T

4   https://www.ft.com/content/8adeca00-2996-11e2-a5ca-00144feabdc0

5   https://blogs.wsj.com/economics/2011/01/31/the-great-stagnation-low-hanging-fruit-and-americas-sputnik-moment/

6   https://governanceai.github.io/US-Public-Opinion-Report-Jan-2019/executive-summary.html

7   https://futurism.com/kurzweil-claims-that-the-singularity-will-happen-by-2045

8   https://www.nickbostrom.com/papers/survey.pdf

9   https://blogs.wsj.com/cio/2018/11/16/the-impact-of-artificial-intelligence-on-the-world-economy/

10 https://www.mckinsey.com/~/media/McKinsey/Featured%20Insights/Artificial%20Intelligence/Notes%20from%20the%20frontier%20Modeling%20the%20impact%20of%20AI%20on%20the%20world%20economy/MGI-Notes-from-the-AI-frontier-Modeling-the-impact-of-AI-on-the-world-economy-September-2018.ashx

11 https://unesdoc.unesco.org/ark:/48223/pf0000246124

12 https://teachertapp.co.uk/marking-like-no-one-watching/

13 Ibid

14 https://ofqual.blog.gov.uk/2020/01/09/exploring-the-potential-use-of-ai-in-marking/

15 https://en.unesco.org/covid19/educationresponse

16 https://www.theguardian.com/education/2020/aug/13/almost-40-of-english-students-have-a-level-results-downgraded

17 Russell, S. (2019). *Human Compatible: AI and the Problem of Control*. London: Allen Lane.

18 https://www.nickbostrom.com/papers/survey.pdf

19 Russell, S. (2019). *Human Compatible: AI and the Problem of Control*. London: Allen Lane.

20 https://dealbook.nytimes.com/2012/08/02/knight-capital-says-trading-mishap-cost-it-440-million/

21 https://futureoflife.org/2017/01/29/dan-weld-interview/

22 https://www.statista.com/chart/17528/countries-which-have-banned-huawei-products/

23 https://www.newstatesman.com/spotlight-america/cyber/2019/11/whats-really-behind-uss-huawei-ban

24 https://www.brookings.edu/blog/future-development/2020/01/17/whoever-leads-in-artificial-intelligence-in-2030-will-rule-the-world-until-2100/

25 Tegmark, M. (2017) *Life 3.0*. London: Allen Lane.

26 https://www.ft.com/content/3467659a-386d-11ea-ac3c-f68c10993b04

27 https://www.thetimes.co.uk/article/only-1-of-cybercrime-prosecuted-claim-lawyers-lzphbxndb

28 https://www.theguardian.com/technology/2014/oct/27/elon-musk-artificial-intelligence-ai-biggest-existential-threat

29 https://www.cityam.com/why-britain-needs-a-minister-for-ai/

Chapter 5 Our teachers

1 Ginott, H. G. (1972) *Teacher and Child*. New York: Macmillan.

2 https://assets.publishing.service.gov.uk/government/uploads/system/uploads/attachment_data/file/686734/Exploring_teacher_workload.pdf

3   https://www.theguardian.com/education/2019/sep/18/25-of-teachers-in-england-work-more-than-60-hours-a-week-study#maincontent

4   https://teachertapp.co.uk/teacher-cash-flow-ideal-lessons-and-how-much-data-do-you-drop/

5   Muller, J., 2018. The Tyranny Of Metrics. Princeton, N.J.: Princeton University Press.

6   https://www.gl-assessment.co.uk/news-hub/press-releases/marking-and-data-still-adding-to-teacher-workload-issues-study-finds/

7   https://teachertapp.co.uk/parents-evenings-parking-collisions-and-two-other-fascinating-findings-from-this-week/

8   Knudsen, C. (1938) 'Ways to Improve the Professional Status of Teachers', *Peabody Journal of Education*, 16 (2), 91–97.

9   https://www.tes.com/news/workload-drives-81-teachers-consider-quitting-union-survey-finds

10   https://www.bbc.co.uk/news/education-43422199

11   https://www.theguardian.com/education/2018/mar/23/best-teacher-in-the-world-andria-zafirakou-build-trust-with-your-kids-then-everything-else-can-happen

12   https://www.theguardian.com/business/2019/jun/28/gig-economy-in-britain-doubles-accounting-for-47-million-workers

13   https://www.nfer.ac.uk/part-time-teaching-and-flexible-working-in-secondary-schools/

14   Ibid

15   https://www.bbc.co.uk/news/education-48595811

16   https://www.nfer.ac.uk/part-time-teaching-and-flexible-working-in-secondary-schools/

17   Ibid

18   https://flexibleteachertalent.co.uk/our-work/f/how-can-we-normalise-flexible-working-in-schools

19   https://www.oecd.org/pisa/pisaproducts/pisainfocus/50328990.pdf

20   https://www.epi.org/publication/teacher-pay-gap-2018/

21   https://www.tes.com/news/watch-englands-teachers-face-more-pupils-less-pay

22   https://www.tes.com/news/englands-teachers-get-developed-worlds-second-biggest-pay-cut

23   https://www.gov.uk/government/news/teachers-set-for-biggest-pay-rise-in-fifteen-years

Chapter 6 The curriculum

1   https://medium.com/solomonkingsnorth/small-is-beautiful-part-one-732239621435

2 https://medium.com/solomonkingsnorth/forget-finland-could-estonia-help-to-reverse-our-dire-sats-and-gcse-results-b56cd746850a

3 https://www.ncbi.nlm.nih.gov/pmc/articles/PMC3792618/

4 https://assets.publishing.service.gov.uk/government/uploads/system/uploads/attachment_data/file/574925/PISA-2015_England_Report.pdf

5 Dweck, C. (2014) 'The power of believing that you can improve', TED.

6 https://medium.com/solomonkingsnorth/the-extraordinary-case-of-mr-yamazaki-18739ebb4980

7 https://medium.com/solomonkingsnorth/forget-finland-could-estonia-help-to-reverse-our-dire-sats-and-gcse-results-b56cd746850a

8 https://www.tes.com/news/international-baccalaureate-global-education

Chapter 7 We treasure what we measure

1 https://www.everydaysociologyblog.com/2012/04/cram-memorize-regurgitate-forget.html

2 https://www.tes.com/news/progress-8-should-not-be-used-measure-individual-class-progress

3 https://www.bristol.ac.uk/policybristol/policy-briefings/progress-8-school-performance/

4 https://www.tes.com/news/exclusive-pressure-schools-forces-government-rethink-progress-8

5 https://leadinglearner.me/2018/03/27/significant-change-to-progress-8-for-2018-outliers-are-out/

6 https://www.tes.com/news/schools-told-scrap-ability-sets-ace-progress-8

7 https://www.theguardian.com/business/2014/may/06/oecd-pisa-tests-education-joy-of-learning

8 https://delano.lu/d/detail/news/lux-partially-withdraws-pisa-assessments/173301

9 https://timesofindia.indiatimes.com/blogs/academic-interest/india-choosing-to-benchmark-itself-on-pisa-a-massive-signal-probably-our-pisa-colleagues-celebrating-more-than-india/

10 https://www.bbc.co.uk/news/business-42781376

11 https://www.telegraph.co.uk/news/2016/12/06/snp-fire-scottish-education-system-records-worst-ever-rating/

12 https://ffteducationdatalab.org.uk/2019/11/should-england-continue-participating-in-pisa/

13 https://www.economist.com/international/2019/12/05/pisa-results-can-lead-policymakers-astray

14 https://www.cambridgeassessment.org.uk/insights/real-finnish-lessons/

15   https://www.cps.org.uk/files/reports/original/150410115444-RealFinnishLessonsFULLDRAFTCOVER.pdf

16   https://ora.ox.ac.uk/catalog/uuid:62b7a22f-d930-4eb0-893d-d703fd9d182d/download_file?file_format=pdf&safe_filename=Complete%2Bthesis&type_of_work=Thesis

Chapter 8 The village

1   http://www.oecd.org/education/EAG2014-Indicator%20D1%20(eng).pdf

2   https://digital.nhs.uk/data-and-information/publications/statistical/mental-health-of-children-and-young-people-in-england/2017/2017

3   https://www.sciencedirect.com/science/article/pii/S0165032716318080

4   https://www.theguardian.com/society/2018/aug/06/hospital-admissions-for-teenage-girls-who-self-harm-nearly-double

5   https://www.thelancet.com/journals/lancet/article/PIIS0140-6736(19)31102-X/fulltext

6   https://youngminds.org.uk/about-us/media-centre/press-releases/teacher-survey-reveals-mental-health-crisis-in-our-classrooms/

7   https://teachertapp.co.uk/what-teachers-tapped-8-may-2018/

8   https://www.bpas.org/about-our-charity/press-office/press-releases/bpas-report-released-on-the-decline-in-teenage-pregnancy-rates/

9   https://assets.publishing.service.gov.uk/government/uploads/system/uploads/attachment_data/file/774866/youth_justice_statistics_bulletin_2017_2018.pdf

10   https://www.bbc.co.uk/news/uk-20863917

11   Ibid

12   https://time.com/5390435/teen-social-media-usage/

13   https://www.pewresearch.org/internet/2018/09/27/a-majority-of-teens-have-experienced-some-form-of-cyberbullying/

14   https://journals.sagepub.com/doi/abs/10.1177/2167696813479780

15   https://assets.publishing.service.gov.uk/government/uploads/system/uploads/attachment_data/file/664855/Transforming_children_and_young_people_s_mental_health_provision.pdf

16   https://www.theguardian.com/education/2019/dec/03/british-schoolchildren-among-least-satisfied-with-their-lives-says-oecd-report

17   https://www.telegraph.co.uk/education/educationnews/11642858/Nicky-Morgan-top-rugby-coaches-to-teach-pupils-grit-and-respect.html

18   https://youngminds.org.uk/media/1428/wise-up-prioritising-wellbeing-in-schools.pdf

19   https://www.theguardian.com/society/2019/apr/29/mental-health-provision-young-people-uk-behind-eu-study

20   https://developingchild.harvard.edu/resources/establishing-a-level-foundation-for-life-mental-health-begins-in-early-childhood/

21   https://epi.org.uk/publications-and-research/access-to-child-and-adolescent-mental-health-services-in-2019/

22   https://developingchild.harvard.edu/resources/establishing-a-level-foundation-for-life-mental-health-begins-in-early-childhood/

23   https://youngminds.org.uk/resources/policy-reports/our-view-on-the-government-s-green-paper/

24   The ten keys, spelling out GREAT DREAM, are Giving, Relating, Exercising, Awareness, Trying out, Direction, Resilience, Emotions, Acceptance, and Meaning (from https://www.actionforhappiness.org/10-keys).

25   http://www.lse.ac.uk/News/Latest-news-from-LSE/2019/g-July-2019/New-soft-skills-training-in-schools-improves-children's-health-and-behaviour

Chapter 9 Learning science

1   Plato (3rd edn. 2007) *The Republic*. Penguin Classics.

2   Cole, M. (2010). Taxi Rides and Cognitive Neuroscience - A Student's Guide to Cognitive Neuroscience (2nd Edition). Jamie Ward (Ed.). 2010. New York: Psychology Press, 453 pp. Journal of the International Neuropsychological Society, 16(5), 945-946. doi:10.1017/S1355617710000937

3   Smith, C. U. M. (2013) 'Cardiocentric Neurophysiology: The Persistence of a Delusion', *Journal of the History of the Neurosciences*, 22 (1), 6–13, https://doi.org/10.10 80/0964704X.2011.650899.

4   Uttal, W. R. (2011) *Mind and Brain: A Critical Appraisal of Cognitive Neuroscience*. MIT Press.

5   Shallice, T. and Cooper, R. (2011) *The Organisation Of Mind*. Oxford: Oxford University Press.

6   Ibid

7   Chase, W. G., & Simon, H. A. (1973). Perception in chess. Cognitive psychology, 4(1), 55-81.

8   https://tomneedhamteach.wordpress.com/2018/09/10/applying-cognitive-load-theory-part-1-overview-and-the-worked-example-effect/

9   https://www.tes.com/news/how-useful-cognitive-load-theory-teachers

10   https://educationinspection.blog.gov.uk/2019/02/13/developing-the-education-inspection-framework-how-we-used-cognitive-load-theory/

11   https://files.eric.ed.gov/fulltext/ED536926.pdf

12   Walker, M. (2018) *Why We Sleep*. Penguin.

13   https://www.bbc.co.uk/news/education-51207415

14   https://www.bbc.co.uk/news/health-39140836

15   http://healthysleep.med.harvard.edu/healthy/matters/benefits-of-sleep/learning-memory

16   https://www.thetimes.co.uk/article/france-gives-tired-pupils-given-extra-hour-in-bed-8jz5d5fgm

17   https://www.itv.com/news/2020-01-30/many-children-own-mobile-phone-by-time-theyre-seven-report-suggests/

18   https://www.motsd.org/cmsAdmin/uploads/blackwell-theories-of-intelligence-child-dev-2007.pdf

19   https://msutoday.msu.edu/news/2020/does-a-growth-mindset-matter-for-success/

20   https://www.tes.com/news/growth-mindset-where-did-it-go-wrong

21   Whittman, G. and Kelleher, I. (2016) *Neuroteach: Brain Science and the Future of Education*. Rowman & Littlefield.

22   https://issues.org/rethinking-the-race-between-education-technology/

23   https://www.learningandwork.org.uk/wp-content/uploads/2019/12/2019-Participation-Survey-Report.pdf

24   https://www.gallup.com/workplace/231668/dismal-employee-engagement-sign-global-mismanagement.aspx

25   https://www.apa.org/science/about/psa/2018/06/motivation

26   Willingham, D. (2010) *Why Don't Students Like School?* San Francisco, CA: Jossey Bass.

Chapter 10 Education 4.0

1   Churchill, W. and Langworth, R. (2012) *Churchill In His Own Words*. London: Ebury.

2   Thiel, P. and Masters, B. (2014) *Zero to One: Notes on Startups, or How to Build The Future*. Penguin Random House.

3   Mazzucato, M. (2018) *The Entrepreneurial State: Debunking Public Vs. Private Sector*. London: Penguin Books.

4   https://www.antonhowes.com/uploads/2/1/0/8/21082490/spread_of_improvement_working_paper.pdf

5   Schwab, K. (2017) *The Fourth Industrial Revolution*. Penguin.

6   Colvile, R. (2016). *The Great Acceleration: How The World is Getting Faster, Faster.* Bloomsbury.

7   Seldon, A. and Abidoye, O. (2018). *The Fourth Education Revolution: Will Artificial Intelligence Liberate Or Infantilise Humanity?* Buckingham: The University of Buckingham Press.